SOFTBALL: SLOW AND FAST PITCH

About the Authors

Marian E. Kneer, Professor Emerita of Physical Education, University of Illinois at Chicago, received her Ph.D. from the University of Michigan. Dr. Kneer has had a long association with softball as a player in four ASA World Softball Championships, a member of the Joint International Rules Committee on Softball, a writer of numerous softball articles for the former Division of Girls and Women's Sports, and as a consultant for several softball filmstrips. She is a member of the Illinois ASA Softball Hall of Fame and the Illinois State University Athletic Hall of Fame. She has had extensive experiences as a high school physical education teacher and as a softball coach. In addition, Dr. Kneer is a physical education curriculum and instruction specialist and is coauthor of the book *Physical Education Instructional Techniques: An Individualized Humanistic Approach,* published by Prentice-Hall. Presently, she is a physical education consultant.

Charles McCord, having achieved success in teaching, coaching, and competitive sports, again joins forces as coauthor with Dr. Kneer in this revision.

After earning his degree from Eastern Illinois University, he both taught and coached for two years at the high school level. For eighteen years he officiated competitive sports on both the high school and college levels. During this time, he has conducted clinics overseas on softball for the men and women of the United States Armed Forces.

Besides his teaching and coaching accomplishments, he managed the nationally famous women's softball team, Lettes, of Caterpillar-Sunnyland and Pekin, Illinois, from 1947 to 1972. During his tenure, the team qualified for the national tournament nineteen times.

Since 1952 he has held the position of State Softball Commissioner for the Illinois Amateur Softball Association and is also the chairperson of the National Hall of Fame Selection Committee. He has held this position since 1958.

Mr. McCord is a member of the Pan-American Committee for Softball and assisted in writing the procedure for selecting the players to represent the U.S. teams. He was elected president of the Amateur Softball Association (ASA) in 1984 and is a member of the Eastern Illinois University and Peoria Area Athletic Hall of Fame, the Illinois ASA Hall of Fame, and the ASA National Hall of Fame.

SOFTBALL: SLOW AND FAST PITCH
Sixth Edition

Marian E. Kneer
Professor Emerita, University of Illinois at Chicago
Illinois ASA Softball Hall of Fame

Charles L. McCord
Illinois State ASA Commissioner
Member ASA Softball Hall of Fame

Boston, Massachusetts   Burr Ridge, Illinois   Dubuque, Iowa
Madison, Wisconsin   New York, New York   San Francisco, California   St. Louis, Missouri

Book Team

Executive Editor *Edward Bartell*
Editor *Scott Spoolman*
Production Editor *Debra DeBord*
Art Editor/Processor *Renee Grevas*
Visuals/Design Developmental Consultant *Marilyn A. Phelps*
Visuals/Design Freelance Specialist *Mary L. Christianson*
Marketing Manager *Pamela S. Cooper*
Advertising Coordinator *Susan J. Butler*
Production Manager *Beth Kundert*

WCB/McGraw-Hill

A Division of The McGraw-Hill Companies

Executive Vice President/General Manager *Thomas E. Doran*
Vice President/Editor in Chief *Edgar J. Laube*
Vice President/Marketing and Sales Systems *Eric Ziegler*
Director of Production *Vickie Putman Caughron*
Director of Custom and Electronic Publishing *Chris Rogers*

President and Chief Executive Officer *G. Franklin Lewis*
Senior Vice President, Operations *James H. Higby*
Corporate Senior Vice President and Chief Financial Officer *Robert Chesterman*
Corporate Senior Vice President and President of Manufacturing *Roger Meyer*

Consulting Editor
Physical Education
Aileene Lockhart
Texas Women's University

Sports and Fitness Series Evaluation Materials Editor
Jane A. Mott
Texas Women's University

Cover photo research and mechanical by Ellen Pettengell Design

Cover image by Superstock

Copyedited by Laurie McGee

Library of Congress Catalog Card Number: 94–70167

ISBN 0–697–15255–3

10 9 8 7 6

Contents

Preface

Although softball is a well-established game, rules, equipment, and strategies do slowly change over time. The sixth edition of *Softball: Slow and Fast Pitch* reflects these changes. In addition the text has been refined, the illustrations have been improved, and a clearer and more in-depth treatment of slow-pitch softball is included.

The purposes of this book are to assist all softball players of any age, beginners to advanced, to acquire the knowledge and skills necessary for playing fast- or slow-pitch softball; to provide instructors, coaches, and managers with substantive information about softball and suggestions for structuring meaningful and productive learning experiences; and to aid students of the game to learn how to umpire and keep score. Emphasis has been placed on skill analysis, error correction, and the values of softball and its place in our culture. Individual and group practice suggestions are included to foster improvement in performance.

Although the purpose of this book is to assist all softball players of any age and skill level, the focus is directed to the college student who has elected to enroll in a softball class for whatever reason.

Self-evaluation questions are distributed throughout the text. They afford the reader typical examples of the kinds of understanding and levels of skill that should be acquired as progress is made toward mastery of softball. The player should not only answer the printed questions but also should pose additional ones as a self-check on learning. Since the order in which the content of the text is read and the teaching progression of the instructor are matters of individual choice, the evaluative materials are not positioned according to the presentation of given topics. In some instances the reader may find that he or she cannot respond fully and accurately to a question without more extensive reading or more playing experience. From time to time the reader should return to such troublesome questions until he or she is sure of the answers or has developed the skills called for, as the case may be.

What Softball Is Like

Enthusiasts need to know about the background of softball, its variations, and the kind of equipment to purchase and how to care for it. In addition, information about the possibilities of participation in tournaments will enhance a player's appreciation of the game.

Instructional Objectives

You will be able to—

1. distinguish softball from baseball,
2. identify the playing areas of an official field,
3. differentiate between fast-pitch and slow-pitch softball,
4. understand the general conduct of a softball game,
5. identify, select, and care for softball equipment, and
6. appreciate the wide acceptance of softball.

Softball is the largest participatory sport in the United States. More than thirty-five million Americans of all ages, sizes, and abilities, and both sexes enjoy playing it informally at picnics, parks, and recreation areas, and formally in a variety of leagues, conferences, and tournaments at interscholastic, intercollegiate recreational, industrial, and professional levels.

Softball is a variation of baseball that was originated by George Hancock of Chicago, Illinois, in 1887 to permit the popular game of baseball to be played indoors. He devised smaller playing dimensions to accommodate the larger and softer ball. The variation became so popular that the indoor game was brought outdoors and became known by a variety of names such as kittenball or mushball. Recreation agencies found the adaptation to be better suited and more appealing to all ages and both sexes than baseball, which required a heavier bat, smaller and harder ball, and a larger playing area. Softball, on the other hand, is played on a smaller diamond with a larger ball and a lighter bat. The pitcher pitches underhand instead of overhand. Base runners may not lead off base in some variations of the game, and a game consists of seven instead of nine innings. These changes provide a sport that is like baseball but can be played in a smaller area by men, women, and children. It has become basically an amateur sport, whereas baseball includes professional as well as amateur play.[1]

1. *Softball, A Game for Everyone* (Oklahoma City: Amateur Softball Association of America, 1977), p. 2.

Softball is a game for everyone. Power is required to hit the ball, yet accuracy in placing the ball so that a fielder cannot reach it can make up for lack of power. The varied playing situations require quick, intelligent decisions. The game calls for individual and team effort. Basic skills used are throwing, catching, running, and hitting. The game demands strenuous effort and yet provides sufficient rest periods. The equipment is relatively inexpensive, and the rules are easily adapted to various playing situations. Softball is one of the safest sports for participants of any age.

Softball has become a popular interscholastic and intercollegiate sport for girls and women. Special rules have been developed for disabled players. The Amateur Softball Association (ASA) is the main governing body for softball in the United States. It has drawn up rules governing play for teams that wish to affiliate and to compete in metropolitan, state, regional, national, and international competition. Many organizations sponsor softball leagues and adopt special rules for their play only.

Types of Games

In general, there are four types of softball: eleven- and twelve-inch slow- and fast-pitch softball and fourteen- and sixteen-inch slow-pitch softball. The playing field, pitching distances, and rules vary for each type of play and for youth, coed, collegiate, and adult play. It is essential that a player have the current year softball rule book to be properly informed of the regulations of the selected type of play. Literally hundreds of national championships are sponsored annually by the ASA and intercollegiate, interscholastic, state, and national agencies.

Playing Field

The softball playing field is the space within which the ball may be legally played and fielded. This space must be clear and unobstructed within the prescribed fence distances and sidelines, which are called *foul lines*. This space is divided into two major areas, the *infield* and the *outfield*. The infield is the area containing the diamond formed by the placement of the bases. There are three bases and a home plate in the infield or diamond. The home plate is the starting point for play. The foul lines extend from home plate through first and third base to the fences. The outfield is the area between the infield and the fences. The distances between home plate and fences and from home plate to the bases vary between slow- and fast-pitch softball, between age levels of play, and even between the gender of the participants.

Fast Pitch

The game of fast-pitch softball requires nine players on a team and ten if a designated hitter is to be used. Each team assigns players to certain defensive positions. These are pitcher, catcher, first baseman, second baseman, third baseman, shortstop,

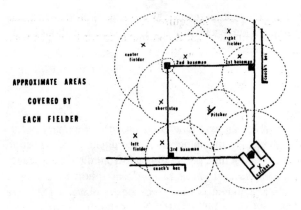

APPROXIMATE AREAS

COVERED BY

EACH FIELDER

Figure 1.1
Diamond and defensive stations (fast pitch).

left fielder, center fielder and right fielder. The designated hitter (DH) does not play a defensive position but rather is assigned to bat for one of the defensive players who does not then bat. The players are stationed on a playing field that has a clear and unobstructed area from home plate to the outfield ranging from a minimum distance of 200 feet for women and maximum distance of 250 feet for males, to a minimum of 150 feet and maximum of 175 feet for boys and girls age ten or under. The batter stands at home plate and tries to hit a ball that is delivered by the pitcher. If the batter succeeds, he or she tries to reach first base and eventually advance around the diamond until returning to home plate. The players in the field try to prevent runners from scoring. Each time a runner crosses home plate, a run is scored. The team with the most runs after seven innings of play is the winner.

Pitching dominates fast-pitch softball when it is played by highly skilled players. The pitcher must deliver the ball underhand. The batter must decide whether or not to swing at the pitch. If the batter does not swing at it, the umpire judges whether the ball was delivered over the plate and between the batter's armpits and the top of his or her knees when the batter assumes a natural batting stance. This area is called *the strike zone*. If the pitch is in the strike zone, a strike is called. If it is not, a ball is called. If three strikes are called, the batter is declared out. If four balls are called, the batter is allowed to take first base. The batter attempts to hit the ball so that it will settle on fair ground in the infield or strike fair ground in the outfield. If the batted ball is hit outside of this area it is in foul territory and is called a foul ball. The first two are counted as strikes. When the ball is hit into fair territory, the batter and all other base runners try to reach as many bases as possible.

The defensive team members play positions within the boundary lines of the field and attempt to put batters and base runners out before they are able to complete the circuit of the bases.

Figure 1.1 illustrates the diamond and the defensive areas covered by each player. Outs occur when the batter strikes out, when a fly ball is caught, when the base is touched with the ball before the runner reaches it when forced to run because of a succeeding runner, and when a runner is touched with the ball before reaching a base. Three outs retire the batting team. The fielding team is then given a chance to bat and to score runs. When each team has had a turn at bat, an inning has been completed.

Slow Pitch

Slow-pitch softball has in recent years shown tremendous growth. The major difference from fast-pitch softball is evident in the name itself. The pitcher is restricted to delivering the ball at a moderate speed with a perceptible arc from the time it leaves his or her hand until it reaches approximately three feet in front of home plate. Base runners may not steal bases, and a team consists of ten or eleven players. The extra players are called short fielder and extra hitter (EH). The short fielder may play anywhere on the field. Extra hitters may not play on defense and may not be used in a coed slow-pitch game. Bunting is illegal. Slow-pitch softball attracts more participants than fast-pitch softball because it is less physically demanding in terms of hitting, throwing, and baserunning.

Slow-pitch was designed to permit more offensive action by making batting easier. However, the tenth player, the short fielder, is usually placed in the outfield to make place hitting more difficult. Although fast-pitch softball may make batting more difficult, a faster pitched ball goes farther when hit, and bunting a pitched ball and stealing bases are allowed, which increases offensive action. The two types of play result in differences in strategy, challenge, and player interests. The major throwing, batting, catching, and fielding techniques are used in both slow-pitch and fast-pitch softball. The slow-pitch playing field is similar to the fast-pitch field, except that the distance from home plate to the fence ranges from 300 feet minimum to 325 feet maximum for super play.

The game of fast-pitch or slow-pitch softball provides enjoyment and challenge for persons of both sexes, all ages, and varied skill levels. A great deal of force and control is necessary to hit or throw the ball accurately. Players must learn to absorb that force to catch or stop the ball. Timing and flow are integral aspects of the game. Timing is needed for executing plays or swinging at the pitched ball. Flow of movement is essential for combining a series of skills for a single execution, such as pitching or executing a double play.

How do slow- and fast-pitch softball compare in the following: number of players, amount of action in the game; delivery of pitches; baserunning; and bunting regulations?

Equipment

The minimum equipment necessary to play softball officially is a ball and a bat. However, players usually wear gloves or mitts depending upon their position. Bases may be makeshift, and official dimensions modified (see figure 1.2).

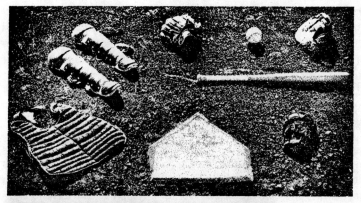

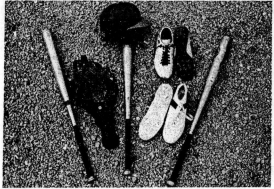

Figure 1.2
Softball equipment.

Bats

The rules permit a variety of materials to be used in manufacturing official bats: wood, laminated wood, plastic, bamboo, and metal. In addition, there are several unofficial plastic bats that are hollow, lightweight, and do not present a hazard to students or to gym floors. A wide selection of bats with differing size grips and barrels should be available. The bat is made of one piece of hardwood or formed from woods bonded together with plastic, bamboo, or metal. The surface must be smooth and free of burrs, rivets, or other hazards. It is not more than thirty-four inches long or more than two and one-eighth inches in diameter at its largest part and has a safety grip of cork, tape, or composition material. A safety knob of a minimum of one-fourth inch protruding at a ninety-degree angle from the handle must be included on all bats. This feature is designed to prevent the bat from slipping out of the hands.

Select a bat that is the proper length, weight, and style for your body build, strength, and type of swing. Generally, short, small players select lighter and shorter bats, and taller and heavier players choose longer and heavier ones. The bat should feel balanced in your hands. It should be heavy enough to add force to the swing but light enough to permit wrist whip action.

A heavy, tapered bat is often used by power hitters. The "bottleneck" bat is used for sharp hits out of the infield or for bunting. Bats made from ash woods tend to be lighter than hickory bats. The aluminum bat is now the most preferred bat because of its durability and low cost. It is often used by players because off-center contacts seem to maintain more power. On the other hand, many players still prefer the wooden bat because they believe they can "whip" it better and it sounds more solid upon contact with the ball.

Balls

Softballs vary in size and thread color according to type of play. The twelve-inch ball is used in both the fast-pitch and slow-pitch game. White stitches are used in men's and women's fast pitch, boys and girls Junior Olympic ages twelve to eighteen fast pitch, and boys ages fourteen, sixteen, and eighteen slow pitch. Red stitches are used for adult men slow pitch and coed slow pitch (male batters only). The eleven-inch ball with white stitches is used in boys and girls Junior Olympics ages ten and under fast-pitch play, whereas the eleven-inch ball with red stitches is used in women's slow pitch, coed slow pitch (women only), boys Junior Olympic age ten and under, and twelve and under slow pitch and all girls Junior Olympic slow-pitch play. The red thread color is thought to aid ball visibility and thus improve batting skill.

The core of the ball is made of long fiber kapok, a mixture of cork and rubber, a polyurethane mixture, or other materials approved by the ASA. It may be hand- or machine-wound, with fine quality twisted yards, and covered with latex or rubber cement. The cover is made from either horsehide, cowhide, synthetic material, or other material approved by the ASA.

Softballs are closely controlled by the rules as to weight, diameter, contents, cover, and stitching. Be certain when buying softballs that they are marked "Official Softball." The brand name of the balls you purchase depends upon personal choice. Most players like to play with a ball that "feels" light; however, these balls often are not durable.

Fleece balls and plastic balls are recommended for primary-age children, but in junior high school, regular fast-pitch softballs should be used. If the ball seems too hard, a rubber-covered, soft softball may be more desirable. Teams should use regulation softballs. Tests are made each year by the Amateur Softball Association Equipment Standards Committee to determine conformity to the rules.

Batting Helmets

All adult fast-pitch and Junior Olympic fast- and slow-pitch offensive players must properly wear approved batting helmets. Helmets on a team are to be of similar color with double earflaps. The helmets must have safety features equal to or greater than those provided by the full plastic cap with padding on the inside.

Gloves and Mitts

There are many styles of gloves and mitts. Mitts do not have fingers. Individual differences in hand size and comfort of the glove will determine the style you purchase. Only the catcher and the first baseman may wear mitts, and the rules spell out the specific regulations concerning their pattern. The webbing of the glove may not be more than five inches. The pitcher's glove must be of one color and not white or gray. Multicolor gloves are unacceptable.

Most players prefer a baseball glove with a large pocket to gloves specially constructed for softball use. Baseball catchers' mitts do not work well for catchers' mitts. Usually, first basemen's mitts are used by catchers. Padding is not too important in softball gloves or mitts, but the softness of the leather is important. Horse-, cow-, or elkhide are excellent leather coverings. The palms should be oiled or greased. At the end of the season, mitts and gloves should be oiled and stored with a ball or a wad of paper wrapped in the pocket.

What kind of accident is the safety knob on the bat designed to protect against?

Masks and Protectors

The rules for fast- and slow-pitch and youth play vary concerning the use of masks and body protectors. Full protection is required for fast-pitch Junior Olympic catchers. They must wear a mask with a throat protector, approved helmet with ear flaps, shinguards that offer protection to the kneecaps, and a body protector. The slow-pitch Junior Olympic catchers are required to wear an approved batter's helmet with ear flaps, or the catcher's helmet and mask. Adult fast-pitch catchers must wear masks with a throat protector.

These protective devices are recommended for slow pitch but not required. Softball masks are much lighter than baseball masks. They can be purchased with sponge rubber padding or with hair padding covered with leather. Both are excellent, and the selection is a matter of individual preference. Body protectors should be made especially for softball and be only waist long. Light-colored duck filled with kapok is the material commonly used for protectors.

For the type of softball you are playing or planning to play, what are the minimum equipment requirements for an official game?

Shoes

Shoes must be worn by all players. A shoe shall be considered official if it is made with canvas, leather, or other similar material. The soles may be smooth or have soft or hard rubber cleats. Adult players in noncoed play prefer to wear spiked shoes for better traction on the playing ground. Metal sole and heel cleats must be less than three-fourths inches. Rounded metal spikes are illegal. No metal, hard plastic, or polyurethane spikes are permitted for youth or coed play.

Bases, Home Plate, Pitcher's Plate

The regulation home plate is five-sided and made of rubber. The pitcher's plate is constructed of wood or rubber; it is twenty-four inches long and six inches wide. The distance of the pitching plate varies from forty-six feet to thirty-five feet from home plate. Consult the rule book for your type of play. Bases covered with canvas or other suitable material are fifteen inches square. They are placed sixty feet apart and are fastened in place.

In official games, home and pitcher's plates are rubber, and the bases are made with a canvas cover. Official play requires that all bases and plates be secured to the ground.

Specific regulations determine whether or not a softball is "official." When is a red-stitched ball used? a ball with a twelve-inch circumference? a ball with an eleven-inch circumference?

The Game Today

For almost one hundred years softball has been a prime recreational and competitive sport in the United States. Today, it has a home in more than fifty countries in the world. Over thirty million adults and youngsters in the United States and over twelve million in other parts of the world play softball. Each summer thousands of tournaments are held sponsored by schools, churches, armed forces, fraternal clubs, recreation agencies, industries, the Amateur Softball Association (ASA), the United States Slow-Pitch Softball Association (USSPSA), and interscholastic and intercollegiate associations. Competition on the international level is growing. Women led the way with the first tournament in Australia in 1965, and men soon followed in 1967 in Mexico. These games are played every four years. It is expected that softball will soon be included as an Olympic sport. Softball is an official sport of the Pan-American Games. Don Porter, executive director of the Amateur Softball Association, states: "There is hardly a man or woman in the United States who didn't at one time play softball."[2] Playing field facilities are insufficient to fill the demand for playing softball, especially slow-pitch softball. Rules are printed in fifteen different languages.

The Amateur Softball Association (ASA) is organized to promote softball and to provide clinics and information designed to improve play as well as to organize tournaments on a local, district, state, regional, national, and world basis. More than 220,000 teams are involved in ASA adult programs for both fast-pitch and slow-pitch softball. Each year more than a thousand invitational and championship tournaments are conducted at all levels of skill and for both sexes. The ASA Youth Program involves more than seven hundred thousand children.

In 1957 the Amateur Softball Association developed a Softball Hall of Fame. Selections are made on the basis of documented evidence of outstanding performance

2. Don E. Porter, "Softball—Past, Present, and Future," *Journal of Health, Physical Education and Recreation* 42 (May 1971): 36–37.

and contributions to the game on a national level. The headquarters for the Amateur Softball Association and the Softball Hall of Fame are located in Oklahoma City, Oklahoma. In addition to the above services the ASA provides the following:

Aids and clinics for umpires, coaches, and players
Assistance in local league organization and play
Publications (rules, guides, monthly newspapers, and national magazine)
Free literature and instructional films

The International Softball Congress (ISC) is another fast-pitch-only organization. It sponsors tournaments with winners advancing to a world playoff and publishes an annual yearbook. The International Softball Federation (ISF) is composed of a group of national softball organizations that coordinate softball development and international competition. ISF encourages growth of softball on a worldwide basis.

The National Association for Girls and Women in Sports (NAGWS) and the National Association for Sport and Physical Education of the American Alliance for Health, Physical Education, Recreation and Dance promote softball in educational institutions. The NAGWS sponsors a Softball Committee that biannually publishes a Softball Guide with instructional articles, officiating information, rules, and media resources. Softball is usually included in the physical education curriculum from elementary school through college.

The National Federation of State High School Sport organizes high school tournaments.

What opportunities are provided in your community for tournament play and for softball clinics?

Several attempts have been made to professionalize the game. An attempt was made for women in the late forties and fifties and again for both men and women in the late seventies. None of these attempts has been successful over an extended period of time.

Language and Lore of the Game

2

Softball is a "people's" game that has endured for almost a hundred years. As such it has developed a history, a lore, and a language.

Instructional Objectives

You will be able to—

1. appreciate and understand the history of softball, and
2. understand and apply common softball terms.

History

The concept of striking an object and reaching a destination before being "put out" can be traced to England. Early games based on this concept were called "Rounders" or "Town Ball." The early colonists adapted "Rounders" into a game called "One Old Cat." Folklore credits Abner Doubleday in 1839 as having scratched the first baseball diamond in the dust at Cooperstown, New York, and outlined general playing rules. It was then, according to legend, that baseball and its many variations started to grow.

Softball is the most famous offspring of baseball, our national pastime. On a Thanksgiving afternoon in 1887 the Chicago Farragut Boat Club devised and played an indoor game similar to baseball. A boxing glove and broom were used as a ball and bat. The afternoon's fun offered a promise, a promise fulfilled by George W. Hancock, a member of the club, who developed rules and equipment. He produced a larger, softer ball and a bat with a smaller batting surface.

Early organization of game play began in Minneapolis, Minnesota. Lewis Rober, a member of the municipal fire department, made the first "kittenball," or softball, by hand. The firemen amused themselves by playing with it in their free time. The first softball league was organized in Minneapolis in 1900, and the first published rules covering the sport appeared in Minneapolis in 1906. During the next twenty years, the game was played both indoors and outdoors. It was called mushball, kittenball, and pumpkinball. Because the game was less dangerous than baseball, women readily took to it. The game was called "softball" by Walter A. Hakanson, a YMCA director from Denver, Colorado, in 1926. That name was officially adopted in 1933.

Since indoor space was not always available, the game began to be played outdoors more and more. Around 1930, Leo H. Fischer and M. J. Pauley of Chicago adapted the game so that it could be played outdoors. They conducted tournaments that were so successful they were able to convince the 1933 Chicago World's Fair to sponsor a national tournament for men and for women.

Thousands of unemployed adults of the 1932–33 Depression years found the game a satisfying way to use excess leisure time. When they finally found employment, they took the game with them and encouraged their employers to sponsor industrial leagues and teams of highly skilled players. The first national tournament was held in Chicago in 1933 for both men and women. Because of this tournament, a need for greater organization became apparent. In 1934, all organizations sponsoring tournaments met and formed the Amateur Softball Association. At the same time a Joint Rules Committee was formed to standardize rules. Previous to the formation of this committee, the National Recreation Association and the American Physical Educational Association published their own set of rules.

The Amateur Softball Association organized softball into city, state, and regional associations as well as industrial, city, coed, and church leagues. Regional champions competed in a national tournament. Early championship teams came from the Midwest. Since that time champions have come from all different parts of the United States. The national fast-pitch men's and women's championship teams compete in a World Championship tournament. Many teams were and still are sponsored by business and industrial concerns. In recent years these teams have been considered national powers:

1. National Health Care Discount. Men's Fast-Pitch. Sioux City, Iowa
2. Riche's Superior. Men's Super Slow-Pitch. Windsor Locks, Connecticut
3. Vernons. Men's Major Slow-Pitch. Jacksonville, Florida
4. Raybestos Brakettes. Women's Fast-Pitch. Stratford, Connecticut
5. Lettuce. Men's Senior Sixteen-inch Slow-Pitch. Chicago, Illinois
6. UPI. Women's Major Slow-Pitch. Cookeville, Tennessee
7. Lewis Daywall. Coed Major Slow-Pitch. Orlando, Florida

During World War II, softball experienced a brief departure from amateur to professional play for some girls and women. It was born out of concern for the restricted baseball activity because of the war. In Chicago, a Women's Professional League was formed, and shortly afterward, P. K. Wrigley gave support to a Midwest version of women's professional play in a game that was essentially a blend of softball and baseball. Both of these attempts died shortly after the end of the war.

Fast-pitch softball dominated the game from 1940 to 1960. The tendency for excellent pitching to result in low-scoring games gave rise to increasing interest in two variations of the game: slow-pitch softball with a regular-size ball and slow-pitch softball with a larger-size ball. These variations prohibited base stealing, required the ball to be pitched slowly, and permitted two extra players. Slow-pitch softball attracts about 70 percent of softball participants because it lessens the impact of the pitcher on the game outcome and lessens the need for speed on the bases. Consequently, the games become more offensive and provide more opportunity for player involvement.

Figure 2.1
Softball Hall of Fame.

In 1992, the ASA sponsored thirty-seven different slow-pitch, nineteen fast-pitch, and two modified-pitch national championships. Each tournament was unique in terms of type of play, gender, and age group. The game continues to grow in participation and interest. International play is conducted in every continent.

The first ASA Slow-Pitch National Tournament for men was held in 1953, the women's followed in 1961, and the men's Super-Slow-Pitch National Championships began in 1981. By 1965, softball was played in more than fifty countries. The first worldwide tournament was held in 1965 for women in Melbourne, Australia. The men followed with their world tournament in Mexico in 1966. It may be seen that women have been an integral part of the game since its inception.

Softball provides physical activity that permits maximum social interaction. It is fun, relaxing, challenging, active, and rarely dangerous. It is no wonder that softball has such wide appeal.

As both baseball and softball were played, experts developed the game by devising certain playing techniques, and some of their inventions resulted in the formation of new rules. Bill Cummings of Massachusetts developed spins on pitches by the skips and turns he observed when flinging clamshells into the ocean. Paul "Windmill" Watson of Arizona developed the circular windup and the fast pitch. John "Cannonball" Baker of Wisconsin invented the figure-eight windup. These developments resulted in increasing the pitching distances and prohibiting some of the windups.

The National Softball Hall of Fame was established by the ASA in 1957 and is located in Oklahoma City, Oklahoma (see figure 2.1). Both men and women players are eligible to be selected. More than sixty members have been inducted, which also includes founders, executives, and umpires. Visitors may view the historical development of the game, see the pictures of great players, and obtain information about their achievements. Some of the famous men in the Softball Hall of Fame are Harold Gears, Sam Elliott, Al Linde, Bernie Kampschmidt, Dizzy Kirkendall, Jim Ramage, Clarence Miller, John Baker, Warren Gerber, Hugh Johnson, Bill West, John Hunter, Tom Castle, Ben Crane, Ray Stephenson, Don Ropp, Jim Chambers, John Spring, Jerry Curtis, Charles Justice, Harvey Sterkel, Robert Kuykendal,

John Anquillare, and Elmen Rohrs. Women members of the Hall of Fame include Amy Peralta, Marie Wadlow, Betty Grayson, Ruth Sears, Nina Korgan, Marjorie Law, Kay Rich, Margaret Dobson, Bertha Tickey, Gloria May, Donna Lopiano, Joan Joyce, Lorene Ramsey, and Carolyn Fitzwater. Slow-pitch "greats" are Myron Reinhardt, Frank DeLuca, Don Rardin, Alberta Sims, Ida Hopkins, Eddie Zolna, and Eddie Finnegan.

As a tribute to these stars, the ASA has built the Hall of Fame Stadium located on the grounds of their headquarters site in Oklahoma City, Oklahoma. It is considered one of the finest softball stadiums in the world.

In addition, the ASA sponsors state Hall of Fames, and the ISC maintains a Hall of Fame in Kimberly, Wisconsin. Many local areas have developed their own softball Hall of Fame for any and all types of play.

Common Softball Terms

Most of the terms used in softball are taken from baseball. In most cases, these terms simply explain the situation or name the person or item. Some of the terms seem to have little relationship to the situation defined, but there is usually some interesting lore about them.

Altered bat   A bat that has been physically changed so that it no longer meets legal standards.

Appeal play   A violation of the rules that must be called to the umpire's attention for a ruling. Appeal situations result from leaving a base before a fly ball is caught, not touching a base, or batting out of order.

Assist   A fielding credit to a player who helps a teammate make a putout.

Away   The number of outs. "Two away" means the same as "two outs."

Backstop   Another name for the catcher and also the term given to a fence behind home plate.

Backup   A position taken by a fielder behind the player attempting to field the ball to possibly play the ball if it gets past the first fielder.

Bag   The base.

Balk   A term applied to making a motion to pitch without immediately delivering the ball to the batter. If a balk is committed, a ball is called on the batter, and the base runners are given one additional base.

Base on balls   When four balls are called on the batter.

Base path   An imaginary path three feet wide on each side of a direct line between the bases.

Bases loaded, or Bases full   Base runners on every base.

Batted ball   A batted ball is any ball that hits the bat or is hit by the bat and lands either in fair or foul territory. No intention to hit the ball is necessary.

Batter-runner   A batter-runner is a player who has finished his or her turn at bat but has not yet been put out or touched first base.

Batter's box   An area on each side of home plate that is seven feet long and three feet wide. The batter must stand within that area when batting.

Battery   The pitcher and the catcher. They are given that name because they really are the "power source" for action.

Batting order   Official sequence in which the batters will appear at the plate to bat.

Bean ball   A ball pitched too close to the batter's head.

Beat out   To reach a base on a slowly hit ball or a bunt.

Blocked ball   A batted or thrown ball that is interfered with by someone not officially in the game.

Blooper   A batted ball that arches over the heads of the infielders and drops just in front of the outfielders.

Bobble   Juggling the ball while attempting to catch it.

Box   The batter's area, the catcher's area, and the coaches' area. All are officially measured and described in the rules.

Box score   The description of the game that is condensed by the use of symbols. This name was given because the scorekeepers are assigned to an area referred to as a box.

Bunt   A weakly tapped ball that is directed toward the foul lines between home plate and first base or home plate and third base.

Catch   A ball that is batted or thrown, which goes directly to the fielder's glove or hand and is controlled.

Catcher's box   The area legally designated behind the batter in which the catcher is confined until the pitcher releases the ball.

Change of pace   The varying of the speed of a pitched ball.

Chopped ball (slow pitch only)   A chopped hit ball occurs when the batter strikes downward with a chopping motion of the bat so that the ball bounces high into the air.

Chopper   A batted ball that bounces high.

Chucker   The pitcher.

Circuit clout   A home run. The batter "clouts" the ball so far that he/she can circle all the bases.

Clean the bases   To hit a home run with base runners on.

Cleanup   The fourth hitter in the batting order. This name is given because he/she is the best hitter and most able to bring runners home.

Coach   A member of the team at bat who stands within one of the coach's boxes on the field to direct the players of his or her team in running the bases.

Count   The number of called balls and strikes.

Crow hop (fast pitch only)   The act of a pitcher who steps or hops off the front of the pitcher's plate, replants the pivot foot, establishing a second impetus (or starting point), pushes off from the newly established starting point, and completes the delivery.

Crowd the plate   Standing close to the plate.

Cut   To swing at the ball.

Cutoff   Interception of a thrown ball made to put out an advancing runner to allow for changing the purpose of the throw if it appears to be unsuccessful.

Cycle   Hitting a single, double, triple, and a home run in one game by one batter.

Dead ball   A ball no longer in play.

Designated hitter (DH)   A player who can only bat for a designated defensive player. (A fast-pitch-only option.)

Diamond   The area formed by the four bases.

Double play   Two outs usually resulting from one batted ball.

Down   Denotes the number of outs—similar to "away."

Earned run   A run that was scored through offensive play rather than an error.

Ejection   An infraction that requires removal from the game by the umpire, whereby the ejected player or coach can no longer participate.

Error   A defensive misplay.

Extra-base hit   A batted ball on which the batter reaches more than one base other than on an error.

Extra hitter (EH)   A player who can only bat. This player does not play or replace a defensive position. (A slow-pitch noncoed game option.)

Fair ball   Any legally batted ball that is touched or that stops in fair territory between home and first or home and third base, or that lands in fair territory and does not cross the foul line until after it passes first or third base.

Fair territory   The part of the playing field within, and including, the first and third base foul lines from home plate to the bottom of the extreme playing field fence and perpendicularly upwards.

Fan   To strike out.

Fielder   Any player of the team in the field.

Fielder's choice   A play in which the fielder elects to put out a base runner rather than the batter.

Fly ball   A batted ball hit into the air.

Force-out   An out occurring when the defensive player in possession of the ball merely touches the base before the runner, who must move to that base because of the batter's becoming a base runner, reaches it.

Foul ball   A ball hit outside of fair territory.

Foul tip   A batted ball that goes directly to the catcher and is caught. A strike is called.

Four bagger   A home run.

Free trip   A base on balls.

Full count   Three balls and two strikes.

Fungo   A ball hit by tossing the ball from the hand and then hitting it. Fungo hitting is used to provide fielding practice.

Grand slam   Home run with the bases loaded. Taken from the bridge term meaning the best you can get.

Groove   The middle of the strike zone.

Grounder   A batted ball that hits the ground as soon as it leaves the bat.

Hit   To take a turn batting or to hit the ball so as to enable the batter to reach first base safely other than on an error or a base on balls.

Hit away   Batter swinging for a hit rather than a bunt.

Hit batsman   A batter hit by a pitched ball.

Hit the dirt   To slide or to pull away from a bean ball.

Hole   Area not covered by a defensive player. Holes result from shifts in positions.

Home team   The team on whose grounds the game is played. If the game is played on neutral ground, the home team shall be designated by mutual agreement or by a flip of a coin.

Hot corner   Third base.

Illegally batted ball   A ball that is struck by an illegal bat or by the batter while outside the batter's box. Batter is called out.

Illegally caught ball   A ball that is caught by the fielder's clothing, cap, or mask. Base runners are allowed two bases on a thrown ball and three on a batted ball.

Infield   Fair territory bounded by and including the base paths.

Infield fly rule   Applies to a situation when a batter hits a fly ball that can be caught in the infield or shallow outfield and runners are on first and second or on all the bases and there are less than two outs. The batter is called out whether the ball is caught or not. Runners may advance at their own risk of being put out if the ball is dropped.

Innings   A division of the game whereby each team has a turn at batting.

Interference   An act of an offensive play that hinders a defensive player's attempt to execute a play.

Keystone sack   Second base.

Lay one down   To bunt.

Lead off   The first batter up at the beginning of the game and/or inning.

Leaping (fast pitch only)   An act by the pitcher which causes that player to be airborne on his or her initial move and push from the pitcher's plate.

Legal touch   A legal touch occurs when a runner or batter-runner who is not touching a base is touched by the ball while it is securely held in a fielder's hand(s).

Line drive   A batted ball that travels in a straight line.

Mask   Device worn by the catcher and umpires to protect their faces against foul balls or the bat.

Obstruction   An act by a defensive player that hinders the movement of an offensive player around the bases.

On-deck batter   The offensive player whose name follows the name of the batter in the batting order. The player shall take a position within the lines of the on-deck circle nearest his or her bench.

Out   The retirement of a batter or base runner during play.

Outfield   The fair territory beyond the infield.

Outside pitch   Pitched ball that misses the strike zone on the side away from the batter. It is an inside pitch if it misses on the side near the batter.

Overrun   To run beyond the base.

Overslide   The act of an offensive player when, as a runner, he or she overslides while attempting to reach a base.

Overthrow   To throw above the baseman or fielder's head.

Pass   A walk.

Passed ball   A legally delivered ball that should have been controlled by the catcher with ordinary effort.

Pick off   To trap a runner off base.

Pinch hitter   A substitute hitter. So named because often the hitter is put in when a team is losing or in a "pinch."

Pinch runner   A substitute who is put in a game to replace a slow or injured runner on base. The replaced runner is then out of the game.

Pitchout   A pitch purposely thrown wide of the plate so that the batter cannot hit it.

Pivot foot   A foot that the pitcher keeps in constant touch with the pitching rubber until the ball is released. Failure to do so results in a ball being called.

Pop-up   A short, high fly in or near the infield.

Protest   A complaint by a team that a playing rule has not been correctly applied. If upheld, the game may be replayed from the point of the error.

Pull hitter   A hitter who tends to hit the ball too soon and then sharply follows through.

Putout   When a batter or base runner flies or is thrown out.

Quick return pitch   A pitch made by the pitcher with the obvious attempt to catch the batter off balance. This would be before the batter takes his or her desired position in the batter's box or while he is still off balance as a result of the previous pitch.

RBI   Runs batted in.

Relay man   A player who catches a ball from another fielder for possible additional play or redirection.

Runner   A player of the team at bat who has finished his or her turn at bat, reached first base, and has not yet been put out.

Sacrifice bunt   Advancing a base runner by forcing out the batter.

Sacrifice fly   A fly ball that is caught, with less than two outs, and which allows a base runner to score.

Scratch hit   A weak hit.

Shoestring catch   A low diving catch by an outfielder. This term is used because the fielder literally catches the ball off his or her shoestrings.

Southpaw   Left-handed pitcher or batter. Most ball fields are laid out with pitcher facing west; thus his/her left hand would face south.

Squeeze   Advancing a runner from third by bunting.

Steal   To advance to another base after the ball leaves the pitcher's hand and before he/she is in position to pitch again.

Straight away   Normal defensive and hitting pattern.

Strike zone   The space over any part of home plate:
   A. (Fast Pitch Only) between the batter's armpits and the top of the batter's knees when assuming a natural batting stance.
   B. (Slow Pitch Only) The strike zone is that space over any part of home plate between the batter's back shoulder and front knee when he or she assumes a natural batting stance.

Stuff   Quality and quantity of the types of pitches used by the pitcher.

Tag   To touch a base with the ball in hand before a runner arrives or to touch the runner with ball in hand.

Texas leaguer   Weak fly that lands safely.

Three bagger   A three-base hit.

Time   The term used by the umpire to order the suspension of play.

Trap   A ball that is caught immediately after it hits the ground.

Triple play   Three outs resulting from one batted ball.

Turn at bat   A turn at bat begins when a player first enters the batter's box and continues until put out or becomes a batter-runner.

Two bagger   A two-base hit.

Wait out   Strategy by the batter employed to ensure hitting only good pitches but especially contrived to obtain a base on balls.

Walk   Occurs when four balls are called on the batter. The batter is then entitled to go to first base.

Wild pitch   An inaccurately delivered pitch that the catcher has little or no chance of stopping.

What actions during a softball game are described by each of these terms: pickoff, blocked ball, fan, triple play?

Offensive Skills

3

Softball is a fast-moving game that requires speed in running, agility in fielding, and accuracy in hitting and throwing. The degree of mastery in applying these essential fundamentals to specific techniques of batting, fielding, throwing, and baserunning will determine the ultimate enjoyment to be derived from playing the game. Since it takes the ball about one-third to one-half second to reach the batter from the pitcher's hand and about three seconds for a runner to run from one base to another in fast-pitch play, it is apparent that the offensive team must develop sufficient skill to bat and run bases with skill, power, and speed. Although slow-pitch play gives the batter a bit more time, offensive skills are still important to develop.

Batting

Instructional Objectives

You will be able to—

1. hit pitched balls into fair territory,
2. bunt pitched balls that will roll slowly in fair territory near the foul line, and
3. analyze batting errors and apply corrective procedures.

No matter how well you can field, run, or throw, your value to a team will be considerably reduced if you do not have ability in batting. If you can't hit, you can't score, and if you can't score, you can't win. There are many different styles of batting. If one style seems to bring more success than another, adopt that style.

The maximum length of an official bat is thirty-four inches, and it may not weigh more than thirty-eight ounces. Select the proper length, weight, and style for your body build and strength. A player should be able to hold the bat at the end of the handle with the nondominant hand and extend it parallel to the ground. If the bat sags downward, a lighter bat is suggested.

Grip

There are three types of grips—long or power, medium, and short or "choke." Which is used is a matter of personal preference, skill, and game situation. Regardless of the length of the grip, the bat is held with the hands together and with the fingers and thumbs wrapped around the handle. Your dominant hand is placed above the nondominant hand. The second joints of the fingers of your top hand should line up somewhere between the second and base joints of the fingers of your lower

LONG GRIP

Long or *power grip*. Hands near knob to increase leverage and to add force or when the pitch is slow.

MEDIUM GRIP

Medium or *average grip*. Lower hand is an inch or two up from the knob to obtain both power and accuracy.

CHOKE GRIP

Choke grip. Lower hand is placed three to four inches from knob to shorten leverage and gain control. Use when place hitting, or the pitcher has a fast, fast ball.

Figure 3.1
Batting grips.

hand. Grasp the bat firmly but relaxed until you begin to swing. The distance between the knob of the bat and your lower hand on the handle influences the amount of power and control. See figure 3.1.

What are the effects on the placement of the hit if the batter typically swings too early? too late? What correction should you make in each case?

Stance

Batters use a variety of stances: close or away, short or deep, open or closed (see figures 3.2, 3.3, and 3.4). Close or away refers to the distance the feet are from home plate. Short or deep refers to the distance the feet are to the front or rear of the batter's box. Open and closed refers to the position of the front foot in relation to home plate. The stance is open if the foot is farther away from the plate than the rear foot and closed, if it is closer. The stance you use should make you feel comfortable and allow you to hit the balls thrown in the strike zone with accuracy and power.

The distance you should stand from the plate can be measured and adjusted by bending slightly from the waist and placing the top of the bat on the outside corner of the plate while holding the bat with your regular grip. You should feel comfortable and balanced.

Figure 3.2
(a) Batting stance; (b) side view of stance; (c) rear view of stance.

Figure 3.3
Batting stances. (a) Close; (b) away.

a   b

Figure 3.4
Batting stances. (a) Short; (b) deep.

Slow Pitch

If the arc of the ball is less than seven or eight feet, it is better to move up and away to avoid "golfing" or "chopping" at the ball.

1. Stand facing the plate, feet parallel with the ground and shoulder-distance apart.
2. Nondominant shoulder and head face the pitcher.
3. Knees should be relaxed and slightly bent.
4. Bat is held off the shoulder.
5. Arms are held away from the body so they are free to move.
6. Forward arm is held fairly level with the ground.
7. Raise back arm a bit to permit better leverage.
8. Eyes on the ball.

The Swing

The key to successful hitting is a well-timed and smooth swing that is consistently executed and accurately centered on the ball. Practice and concentration are needed to always "hit downward and through the ball."

There are many different styles of batting. However, the stride, pivot, and arm action are crucial to successful hitting.

1. Shift weight back as the pitch is released and take a low stride forward about eight to twelve inches with lead foot. The timing of this action depends on the expected speed of the ball. Keep the rear foot firm. Do not transfer weight forward until the bat begins to move forward.

Slow pitch—short in box.

Figure 3.5
The swing.

2. Pivot on the ball of the rear foot.
3. Rotate the hips upon completion of the stride and keep eyes on the ball.
4. Bring hands and bat forward and extend the forward arm as you snap the wrists just before contact with the ball, then roll hands over.
5. Hit through the center of the ball as you bring the bat around in a full follow-through.
6. Keep the hips, shoulders, and bat as level as possible.

The swinging action is like a coiling and uncoiling around a central axis, the spine. The swing is a rhythmical progressive movement starting with the pivot of the hips and shoulders, continuing with the arms and wrists. This coiling and uncoiling along with the back arm provides the power while the forward arm gives guidance to the swing. The rear leg supports the initial unleashing of the power and the front leg becomes the support for the transfer of power behind the ball. See figure 3.5.

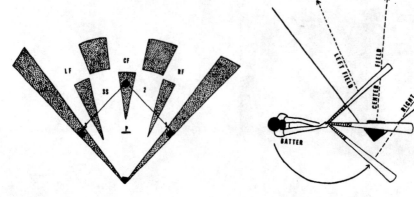

Figure 3.6
Place-hitting areas.

Figure 3.7
Place-hitting techniques.

Safety

Batting has two major safety hazards: being hit by the pitched ball and hitting someone with the bat. The former requires absolute alertness by the batter to avoid being hit. The use of a batting helmet is increasing to avoid injuries to the head from a pitched ball. The latter hazard requires the batter to develop the habit of dropping the bat rather than throwing it. Spectators and other players except the team on the field should be kept at least twenty feet from home plate.

Place Hitting

The number or position of base runners as well as the position of the infield often leaves "holes" or openings between the fielders. A clever hitter knows how to bat into that area. Effective placements of the batted ball can be achieved by adjusting the time that the ball is hit, the position of the feet, and the follow-through of the bat. See figures 3.6 and 3.7.

If you wish to bat the ball to the left side of the field, try to contact the ball in front of the body to shorten the arc of the swing. Your wrists should break sharply, causing a forceful follow-through to "pull" the ball to the side on which you are hitting. To hit the ball to center field, try to contact the ball directly opposite your body and follow through naturally. To hit the ball to right field, try to contact the ball a little past the center of the body; let your follow-through angle the bat to right field. It is also possible to achieve placement of the ball by adjusting your stance, but this method permits the defense to become aware of your intentions and thus take preventive measures. If the pitcher is extremely fast or deceptive, it may not be possible to control the placement of the ball by these measures. In such situations the batter should "go with the pitch." Going with the pitch means that if the ball is outside, it is hit to that side of the field. To hit a long fly ball, grip the bat with a long grip, swing with full force, and try to follow through slightly upward. To avoid hitting a ground ball, strike only at pitches above the waist.

Figure 3.8
Hit-and-run play.

When the pitcher has a great deal of speed, "choke" your grip on the bat to shorten the arc and permit a faster swing. Since this action results in decreased leverage, the power behind the ball will be lessened, but the accuracy of the hit will be increased.

Place-hitting ability is a definite asset to a team. Every good player should develop skill in this advanced technique.

Hit-and-Run

This technique is used to advance a base runner two or more bases, and at the same time it permits a ground ball, which normally would be fielded, to become a base hit. The hit-and-run play is most often used when there is a runner on first base, as in figure 3.8. As soon as the ball leaves the pitcher's hand the runner on first base runs full speed to the next base. This action forces the second baseman to move to cover second base, thereby opening up a defensive "hole." The batter tries to place the ball into the "hole." Whenever this play is attempted by the offensive team, a gamble is taken that a sharp line drive will not be hit directly to a fielder, which would result in a double or triple play. Hit-and-run skill is difficult to master.

Bunting—Fast-Pitch Only

Bunting is an essential skill for any fast-pitch softball player. A bunt is a batted ball that is not hit with a full swing. The bat is not swung at the ball but is placed in the way of the ball and allowed to "give" slightly in the hands, thus causing the ball to lose force. This action allows the ball to be placed approximately ten to twenty feet from the plate and as near the base line as possible.

The ball is bunted to advance a base runner or as an attempt to get a base hit. Bunting to advance a base runner is called *sacrificing*. The sacrifice bunt draws the first baseman, pitcher, and third baseman in toward the plate to field the ball, which

Figure 3.9
The grip.

forces the ball to be thrown to first base, thus permitting the base runner to advance. A variation of the sacrifice bunt is the *squeeze bunt,* which is designed to score a base runner from third base. There are two techniques for bunting for a base hit: *drag bunting,* and *push bunting.* Each of these requires surprise, proper placement, and a fast sprint to first base to be successful. The drag bunt is placed along the first base line as the batter begins to run to first base. Because of this placement, drag bunting is best executed by left-handed batters. The push bunt is placed between the incoming fielders with enough speed to force the ball by them.

A great deal of the success of the bunt depends on the surprise element; a batter therefore must not assume the bunting position until the ball is about to leave the pitcher's hand. There are three bunting positions for the body.

The traditional bunting stance calls for the batter to square around by moving the rear foot in line with the front foot so that the feet are about twelve to eighteen inches apart just as the pitcher begins delivery. The top hand on the bat is moved upward behind the bat. See figure 3.9. *Angle* bunting has become more popular because the batter tends to pop up less, can get into position faster, and gets a faster start to first base.

Sacrifice Bunt

See figures 3.10, 3.11, and 3.12.

1. Stand near the front of the batter's box.
2. Move the rear foot in line with the front foot about twelve to eighteen inches apart as the pitcher begins the delivery.
3. Face the pitcher, arms extended forward, bat held at the top of the strike zone, knees and hips slightly bent with weight on both feet.
4. Drop the bat *on top* of the ball to ensure a grounded hit.

Angle Bunting

1. Stand in front of the batter's box, pivot on the balls of the feet and shift most of the weight to the front foot, bend the body forward and relax the knees, position the front feet very close to the plate and hold the head directly behind the bat.
2. Hold the bat at a forty-five degree angle at all times, bring the bat head in front of the plate and face, and keep it over the plate.

Figure 3.10
Stance for sacrifice
bunting.

Figure 3.11
Side view of stance for
sacrifice bunting.

Figure 3.12
Rear view of stance for
sacrifice bunting.

Figure 3.13
Angle bunting with hands
apart.

Figure 3.14
Angle bunting with hands
together.

3. Hold the top hand a little more than halfway up the bat with both hands
   together or slightly apart (see figures 3.13 and 3.14), hold the bat loosely with
   the top hand to control resistance or give when the ball hits the bat to "kill" the
   forward speed of the ball, and bend the elbows to keep the bat about one-half
   arm length away from the body.

The ball is directed by the bottom hand. To place the ball down the first base
line, push the bottom hand out and away from the body but maintain the forty-five
degree angle. To place the ball down the third base line, pull the bottom half of the
bat toward the body, keeping the forty-five degree angle.

Figure 3.15
Drag bunt.

Figure 3.16
Push bunt.

Drag Bunt

See figure 3.15.

1. Move your feet and arms as they normally move for a full swing.
2. Slide the top hand six to eight inches up the handle just before the ball reaches the plate.
3. Stride toward first base as the ball is contacted.

Push Bunt

See figure 3.16.

1. Move hands and feet as for a drag bunt.
2. Reduce the amount of give and push the ball with enough force between the fielders.

From your observation of softball games, toward which direction do the majority of the hits travel? Do you know why it is preferable to place-hit by adjusting your timing rather than your stance?

Problem	Causes	Corrections
No power	Grip choked	Use medium or long grip.
	Hitting off rear foot	Shift weight forward as bat swings forward.
	No wrist snap	Uncock wrist as ball is contacted.
Missing ball	Swinging too late	Use choke grip.
	Swinging too early	Use medium or long grip.
	Lack of concentration	See bat hit the ball.
Ball hit too far to batter's side	Early swing	Long or medium grip
	Forward foot moved backward	Shorten stance and step toward pitch.
Ball hit too far to side away from batter	Late swing	Choke or medium grip
	Forward foot moved toward plate	Lengthen stance and step toward the pitch.
Ball popped up	Swing is late	Swing sooner or faster.
	Swinging upward	Level swing
	Dropping the shoulder	Keep shoulders level.
Ball hit into ground	Chopping downward	Level swing
Bunt goes too far	Dominant hand not giving	Relax dominant hand and recoil arms.
Bunt popped up	Hitting high pitches	Hit only waist-high or lower pitches.
	Not pushing downward	Follow-through downward.

   Positioning the bat at the top of the strike zone ensures hitting the ball downward with the bottom portion of the bat. The batter lowers the level of the bat by bending the knees and hips while keeping the arms extended. The bat should be angled downward to the left, the center, or to the right, depending on where you wish to place the bunt. Low outside pitches are the easiest to bunt. High, inside pitches are extremely difficult to bunt because the bat must be brought upward, resulting in a tendency to hit up, rather than down on the ball.

Fake Bunting

A fake or slap bunt is often attempted to pull the defense in toward the batter to help a base runner steal or to permit the batter to place-hit the ball in the defensive position vacated. Preferably, the ball should be batted just over the first or third

Figure 3.17
Batting tee.

baseman's head or into the area vacated by the second baseman or shortstop when he/she has moved to cover a base. When you are going to bluff or bunt to facilitate a base hit, deliberately move into bunting position but do not hit the ball. On the next pitch, momentarily move into bunting position and then bring the bat quickly back for the backswing and swing forcefully forward at the ball. If you are faking a bunt to help a runner steal, simply move into bunting position but do not bunt the ball. This action causes the infield to draw in and forces the shortstop to move to cover second or third, depending on which base is being attempted.

Practice

All practice, whether pursued individually or in a group, should be directed at achieving certain goals such as placement, power, level swing, stride, and concentration.

Individual

Bat Swinging Assume proper stance and visualize the ball coming to various corners over the plate. Attempt to swing to hit the ball.

Swing the bat while looking at yourself in the mirror. Check your stride, position of arms, and level of swing.

Swing two or three bats for a short period of time to build arm strength and thus increase the power of your swing.

Repeat the above exercises while using bunting technique.

Batting Tee Swing at a ball on a batting tee. If you cannot obtain one for practice, make one by attaching a ten-inch metal tube to a wooden base. Extend the tube to normal batting height by attaching a rubber radiator hose to it. The ball should be hit slightly ahead of the plate. See figure 3.17.

Figure 3.18
Pepper practice.
(F = fielder,
H = hitter)

Adjust the tee position and adjust follow-through to practice place-hitting at various targets.

When practicing with a batting tee, try to send five successive hits to the left side of the field, five to the center, and five to the right. Can you score three out of each five? four out of five? five out of five?

Group

Group practice gives you the advantage of practicing under the watchful eye of an expert who can observe your mistakes and give you advice on how to overcome them.

Regular Pitcher The best batting practice is against a regular pitcher. Practice swinging at balls pitched to certain target spots. Include concentrated placement, power, and bunting practice.

Pitching Machine Adjust the machine to pitch the ball at various speeds and targets.

Pepper Two hitters stand about fifteen to twenty feet in front of the group and practice hitting balls thrown or pitched by members of the group in rapid succession. Additional balls may be added. This practice is excellent for training the eyes to follow the ball. The ball should be chopped downward to hit the ball directly back to members of the group. See figure 3.18.

Evaluation

A good way to evaluate batting is to utilize a checklist (see figure 3.19) to determine accuracy of form, but more importantly, the best measure is your batting average. You can figure it by dividing the total number of hits you have made by the total number of times you have been at bat. A batting average of .300 or more is considered excellent.

Batting Evaluation		
Name _____ Date _____		
Key: 5 = Excellent; 4 = Very Good; 3 = Average; 2 = Fair; 1 = Poor		

Item	Rating	Comments
1. Ready Position	5 4 3 2 1	
2. Bat Position	5 4 3 2 1	
3. Swing	5 4 3 2 1	
4. Follow-through	5 4 3 2 1	
5. Weight transfer	5 4 3 2 1	

Figure 3.19
Batter evaluation form.

Baserunning

You will be able to—

1. run efficiently and swiftly to first base and to other bases after becoming a base runner,
2. slide on close plays to avoid being tagged,
3. lead off base to gain a jump on advancing to another base, and
4. steal the next base (fast pitch only).

Softball games are often decided by one run. Alert, aggressive, intelligent baserunning often can make the difference between winning or losing. If you are playing on a team and have coaches at first and third bases, allow the coaches to assist you in determining your baserunning actions. Always know where you are and what the situation is relative to other base runners, number of outs, score of the game, count on the batter, and throwing ability of the defensive team.

Running to First Base

See figure 3.20.

1. Push off on forward foot (left, for right-handed batters).
2. Step forward with right foot.
3. Run as fast as possible in a straight line and touch the base with either foot.
4. Do not break stride to look at the ball unless it is behind you or you have no coach.
5. Run full speed over first base if a play is expected there, pull up as soon as possible in event of an overthrow to enable advancing.

Figure 3.20
Takeoff to first base.

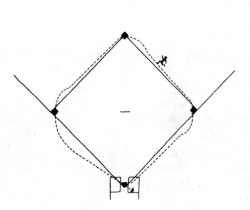

Figure 3.21
Rounding the bases.

Figure 3.22
Touching the base.

6. Curve your run to round the bag if the play is away from first base and touch the inside corner of the bag with your left foot.

Running to Bases beyond First Base

1. Turn out to the right several feet before reaching first base by leaning to the right and taking a couple of steps at an angle away from the foul line (see figure 3.21).
2. Plan to touch the inside corner of the bag without slowing down as you change directions.
3. Touch the bag with either foot as you round the bag, but be prepared to stop if it seems unlikely that you will be able to make it to second base.
4. Straighten out run toward the next base.
5. Continue to curve out several feet before each base you intend to round.
6. Run straight to a base to which the play is to be made.
7. Touch the inside corner of the bag with your left foot and cross your right foot toward the next base. (See figure 3.22.)

Sliding

A good base runner should slide on close plays except when running from home to first base. A slide has two advantages. First, it will stop your run without causing you to lose speed; second, it will give the infielder a small target to touch if it is a tag play. There are four basic types of slides: straight-in, bent-leg, headfirst, and hook.

When sliding try to:

1. not slow your speed during your approach to a base,
2. begin sliding about ten to fifteen feet from the base, depending on your skill, size, and speed.

Safety

1. Never change your mind while in the act of sliding.
2. Avoid sliding without proper protection for your legs.
3. Slide to avoid contact with the baseman.

The *straight-in slide* starts about ten feet from the bag. Lean away from the base and lift up either leg while momentarily extending the other leg downward to the ground. This action will cause the bottom leg to skid along the ground. To prevent the spikes from catching, the skidding leg should immediately be bent at the knee and the extended leg lifted well off the ground. The arms do not come in contact with the ground.

The *bent-leg slide* is executed to stop your speed at a base but allows you to get back on your feet immediately to proceed to another base if possible. Choose this slide if you are unsure about the accuracy of the throw or the closeness of the play. The bent-leg slide is like the straight-in slide except that it is started nearer the base and the backward fall is checked. The nonsliding leg is bent at the knee instead of extended. As soon as the skidding leg touches the base, the weight is brought forward by thrusting the arms forward, thus pulling the body up and shifting the weight to the top leg, which is bent and ready to brace your next running step with the unweighted sliding leg (see figure 3.23).

The *headfirst* slide has increased in popularity despite its potential for upper body injury, because it provides an extremely small tag area. The slide begins about eight feet from the bag. Lean forward toward the base, extend the arms, and catch your weight on the heels of the hands and chest. Keep your head up. Lean forward toward the base by dropping the head and shoulders. Push off with one leg and land on the stomach, abdomen, and thighs to glide along the ground. The hands and arms should be extended toward the base. Bend the knees so that the feet do not drag along the ground. Keep the head back and hands up to avoid injuring them (see figure 3.24).

The *hook slide* is used to avoid a tag by the infielder. The sliding foot barely touches the corner of the bag away from the fielder, and the body falls away from the base. This action allows a very small part of the body to be touched by the ball. The takeoff for a hook slide may be with either foot. Again, the weight is thrown

Figure 3.23
Bent-leg slide.

Figure 3.24
Headfirst slide.

backward, but both feet are bent sideways to prevent the spikes from catching. As the touching foot approaches the bag, the upper part of the body and the nonsliding leg are twisted away from the fielder (see figure 3.25). Once you make a decision to slide, never change your mind! If you change your mind, your spikes might catch the turf and could cause a leg injury.

As a base runner, what information should you have in mind at all times to make the most of your opportunities to advance?

Figure 3.25
Hook slide.

Figure 3.26
Conventional leadoff stance.

Figure 3.27
Rolling-start leadoff.

The Leadoff

Once you have gained a base, you of course will want to reach the next base. Until the heel of the pitcher's foot crosses the front edge of the pitcher's plate as the pitch is made, you must stay on your base. You may not lead off in twelve-inch slow-pitch softball. It is important, however, that you be ready to run. A good leadoff is essential for advancing to another base, either by stealing (fast pitch only) or by advancing on a batted ball.

An effective stance is crucial to the success of a good leadoff. See figures 3.26 and 3.27. The left foot is placed on the inside edge of the base; the other foot may be placed either a step in front or a step behind the left foot. The latter method is used to get the body in motion before the ball leaves the pitcher's hand. A stride is taken as the pitcher's arm starts forward, but the runner must be careful not to leave the base before the ball is released. This stance should not be used in slow-pitch softball. Regardless of the method, the body faces the next base, knees are flexed, and the weight is on the forward foot. Arms are bent and held free of the body, ready to generate momentum. The runner takes two or three steps, stops, and returns if the ball is not hit. The body should be kept under control. When on third base, lead off in foul territory to avoid being called out for being hit with a batted ball.

Strategy

Successful baserunning requires quick and intelligent decisions. Assess the situation.

Force Out, Less Than Two Outs

—on a grounder, run as hard as possible and slide to break up a possible double play.
—on a fly ball, if you can advance, tag up until the ball is caught and leave immediately for the next base.
—on a low line drive that could be caught, go halfway up the base path so that you can advance if not caught or return if it is caught.

Force Out, Two Outs

—on contact with the ball, run hard to next base.
—on full count to batter, run as soon as the ball leaves the pitcher's hand.

Non–Force Out, Less Than Two Outs

—on second base, advance to third if ball is grounded behind you. If grounded in front of you, hold up until the ball is thrown to first base and then attempt to reach third base.
—on third base, tag up on fly ball immediately and score if possible. Hold up if grounded until the ball goes through or is thrown to first base.

As a base runner, what should you do in each case: when a low line drive is hit; on a grounder; on a fly ball?

Stealing

Stealing a base is legal only in fast-pitch softball. It enables a team to get runners into scoring position without using a sacrifice out. Furthermore, the threat of stealing often unsettles the defense and causes errors.

A successful base stealer must be fast and alert to conditions that may enhance the success of the steal. Study the pitcher and the catcher, and watch the infielders for weaknesses that may enhance the success of an attempted steal. It will help you to steal a base if the catcher has a weak throwing arm or tends to

Problem	Causes	Corrections
Slow start from plate or base	Striding too far on the first step	Take short, digging steps.
	Not keeping weight low	Don't look at ball; keep head down.
Sliding too early	Misjudging beginning distance	Place markers to the side of sliding area for practice.
Sliding too late	Indecision	Plan to slide and do it.

ignore your leadoff, or if the infielders seem to be slow to protect the base you seek. Regardless of these weaknesses, if a coach is not giving directions, the following should be considered before attempting to steal:

1. Game score
2. Pitcher's ability
3. Number of outs
4. Ability of succeeding batters
5. Inning you are playing

If you plan to steal the next base, it is important that you do not reveal your intent before the heel of the nonpivot foot crosses the front edge of the pitcher's plate as the ball is delivered so that you will not alert the defensive team. As soon as the foot crosses the pitcher's plate, lower your body, accelerate with short, digging steps and lengthen to full stride until the base is reached. Be prepared to slide.

Delayed Steal

This is a risky play and should be attempted only by swift runners. Lead off the base as usual. If the catcher does not force you back, immediately take off at full speed for the next base as soon as he/she starts to throw the ball to the pitcher. This type of steal can be most effective if there are less than two outs and runners are on first and third bases. The runner on first runs about halfway to second and stops or slows down, deliberately tempting the catcher to throw. If the ball is thrown to second, the runner on third base breaks toward home at full speed. If the ball is not thrown to second, the first-base runner can take second base unchallenged.

Safety

Baserunning can be one of the most dangerous aspects of softball play. You should follow these suggestions:

1. Be aware of fielders and attempt to avoid collisions.
2. Contact the corner of the base away from the baseman whenever possible to avoid bumping him.

Practice

Individual

Actual Baserunning Practice overrunning first base; then, making the turn; then, running to first and second bases; then running from first to third; and finally, running all the way. Carry a stopwatch. Try to improve your time.

Starts Swing bat and take off to full stride. Repeat several times. Stand on base and take off to full stride.

Sliding Slide on a smooth surface indoors such as a gymnasium floor to a loose base in your stocking feet only. Then try grass; then use a sand pit; and finally, slide on the dirt. Wear protective clothing.

Group

Baserunning Run in pairs to the various bases. Time each player's run.

Stealing Place base runner on first base. Have the pitcher pitch and have the catcher attempt to throw the runner out.

Starts Base runner assumes leadoff stance, leaves on signal, stops on whistle, and returns.

Evaluation

Develop a checklist to evaluate starts, leadoffs, and slides. Keep a record of the attempted steals, and divide the successful attempts into the total attempts to secure the percentage of successful attempts. Time each player's running speed to the various bases.

Defensive Skills

4

The shortness of the base paths and the size of the ball give the offensive team an advantage. Consequently, good softball play requires good defensive play. Every player needs to possess skill in fielding ground balls, catching fly balls, and the ability to throw with speed and accuracy. In addition, knowledge of where to throw and when and how to protect a base is vital to good defensive playing ability.

Fielding

Instructional Objectives

You will be able to—

1. catch fly balls in both the infield and outfield,
2. field ground balls and throw out a runner,
3. receive throws and tag out a runner,
4. plan ahead so that cutoff plays, backing up, and base covering are executed.

Catching fly balls, stopping balls hit on the ground, and catching throws are the basic skills needed for good fielding. In all cases, common principles govern the proper fielding of the ball.

Stance

Whenever you are in a defensive position, you must be alert and ready. Figure 4.1 illustrates the proper waiting or ready position. Infielders should set with their arms barely off the ground by bending the legs and extending their arms. Outfielders should set about halfway between the infielders' ready stance and normal standing.

1. Feet are comfortably spread.
2. Body faces batter, and eyes are fixed on ball.
3. Knees and hips are bent.
4. Weight is on balls of both feet.
5. Keep the glove out in front, wide open, and facing the batter.

The ready position is assumed as the ball leaves the pitcher's hand. The defensive fielders must constantly watch the batter, not the pitcher, and react immediately to batted balls; they must track the ball vigilantly.

Figure 4.1
Waiting positions.

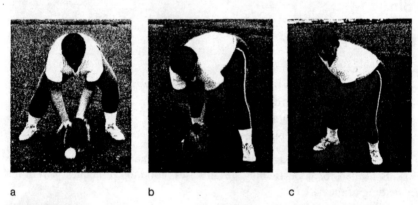

a   b   c

Figure 4.2
Fielding the ball. (a) Lining up the ball; (b) trapping the ball in the glove; (c) moving the hands to a throwing position.

It is important that you stay relaxed throughout your fielding attempt. If the ball is hit or thrown softly, or shallow, or to the left or right, move diagonally toward it. Conversely, if it is hit or thrown sharply or deeply to the left or right, move diagonally backward. The speed of your movement depends on the exact speed of the ball and the distance it is from you.

Catching the Ball

See figure 4.2.

Catching a softball requires similar basic techniques:

1. Move the body so that it is in line with the ball.
2. Watch the ball into the glove or mitt.

Figure 4.3
Judging a fly ball.

3. Catch the ball in the pocket of the glove or mitt.
4. Trap the ball into the glove or mitt with the throwing hand to help secure it and to allow a quick grip on the ball for the return throw.
5. Move the glove or mitt toward the body as the ball enters the pocket to absorb the impact of the ball. This is called *giving*.
6. Place the fingers of the glove or mitt upward, if the ball is above your waist, and downward, if below the waist.
7. Keep your throwing hand protected behind the glove or mitt for safety.

Fly Balls

When a *fly ball* is hit, move at the crack of the bat in the direction of the ball. Run as fast as you can so that you can be there in time to wait for it, if at all possible. The speed, direction, height, and effect of the wind on the ball should be determined immediately, and a judgment should be made as to about where the ball can be caught. This judgment is made as you are already on the move to that spot. The sound of the bat against the ball, as well as the visual sighting of the speed of the ball, will give you some immediate information as to where to go. If the ball is hit high, you will have a little more time to get there than if the ball is hit low. Be prepared for final adjustments while waiting for the ball to descend if a high wind is blowing. (See figure 4.3.)

If the ball is going to come down behind you, turn to whichever side is necessary, using whatever footwork comes naturally. Look over your shoulder at the ball as you move backward and sideways for it. Try to avoid having to turn your back on the ball. If the speed of the ball requires a more rapid move backward, however, do turn your back and run back. Try to look back at the ball to continue to track it.

Be sure you are back far enough to catch the ball, because it is easier to take a step or two forward than it is to back up. As the ball descends, get ready for the

Figure 4.4
One-hand catch of fly ball.

Figure 4.5
Moving back to catch a fly ball.

ball by standing with your legs comfortably spread, with the leg opposite to the throwing arm slightly ahead so that you are ready to throw. Try to reach about head high for the ball to save time in making the catch; when running for the ball, have your glove out ready to catch it. (See figures 4.4, 4.5, and 4.6.)

Always try to be prepared to return the ball quickly. When there are base runners and if time permits, attempt to run or "loop" back a few steps behind where you plan to catch the ball so that you will be moving toward the base that you expect to be throwing to as you catch the ball. Improvements in gloves have increased the use of catching fly balls with one hand. Such a practice increases range and stability.

The presence of the fence and sun present difficult encounters for the fielder. The effects of the sun can be avoided by trying to turn the body to look away from

Figure 4.6
Moving in to catch a fly ball.

it. Use sunglasses if possible and/or use the hand or glove to shield the sun. You can avoid running into a fence by reaching back with the nonglove hand to gauge your distance from the barrier. (See figures 4.7 and 4.8.)

Try to catch every ball in your area unless by catching a foul you would allow a base runner to advance or score in a close game. As soon as you know you can catch the ball, warn your teammate by shouting, "I have it!" If you hear this signal from someone else before you call it, immediately move away from the ball to avoid collision with the teammate who is fielding the ball. Collisions may result in errors or serious injuries.

Ground Balls

Ground balls seldom are affected by a wind factor, but the surface of the playing field often causes the ball to bounce erratically, which causes difficulty in judging where to catch it. Just as in fielding fly balls, the decision based on the sound of the crack of the bat against the ball and the speed and direction of the ball must be made immediately so that no time is wasted in getting in the proper place to stop the ground ball. Since the batter is not out on a ground ball until the ball reaches the base he/she is attempting to reach, move quickly toward the ball. Avoid letting the ball "play you" by not moving backward on it. Shift your weight forward, pivot toward the side the ball is coming from, and run in a low position to save time in bending down for the ball at the last second. Time your run so that you can catch the ball just after it starts its bounce. This timing will avoid erratic twists and will save time. Use crossover steps (see figure 4.9) when you must run a considerable distance and sidesteps when the distance is short. Crossing the legs when moving laterally will generate the needed speed to get to the ball. Sidestepping is slower but surer for reaching balls that are hit closer to you and thus will ensure greater control. As the ball nears you, stop running and brace yourself by spreading your feet comfortably.

Figure 4.7
Protecting against the fence.

Figure 4.8
Protecting against the sun.

Figure 4.9
Crossing over for a grounder.

There are eight procedures that should be used for stopping ground balls. (Study figure 4.10.)

1. Place your glove-hand foot forward.
2. Bend your knees and hips low so that your hands touch the ground when hanging relaxed.
3. Move so that you are in line with the ground ball.
4. On a roller, stop the ball inside your glove-hand side foot.
5. On a hopper, pick the "best hop," preferably below waist high.
6. Watch the ball into the glove, and secure the ball with the throwing hand.
7. Protect the throwing hand by fielding only with the glove hand.
8. Protect the fielded ball by immediately placing the throwing hand over the ball and gripping it so that a throw may easily be made if necessary.

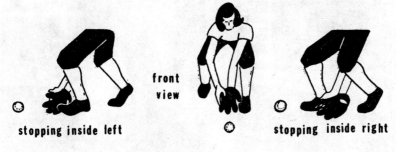

front
view

stopping inside left

stopping inside right

Figure 4.10
Fielding a ground ball.

Figure 4.11
Backhand pickup.

In fielding ground balls, when should you use crossover steps, and when are sliding steps preferable?

There are two difficult pickups to be made when fielding ground balls: *backhand* and *still* balls. A backhand pickup is necessary when the ball is impossible to reach in proper position on the nonglove side. In this situation, cross the glove and side foot over in front of the nonglove foot, and pivot body so that the back is toward the ball. Now reach for the ball with the glove hand while turning the glove over to smother it. Keep your eyes on the ball and your body low. As the ball enters the glove, bring the nonglove foot forward, and put the base hand into the glove to prepare for the throw (see figure 4.11). Speed is needed to field a stopped ball. Pick

a   b

Figure 4.12
Covering base. (a) Waiting; (b) catching.

it up with the bare hand, watch the ball, stay down, pick it up in front of the non-glove foot and shift weight to the glove foot as you throw.

Always try to stop the ball with the glove-side foot forward and near the inside of that foot. This action allows better viewing of the ball and places the body in a good balanced position for throwing. If the ball is hit slowly, charge the ball by cutting diagonally to the right or left if necessary. If the ball is hit with great speed, move diagonally backward to the right or left. If there is not enough time to get the glove-side foot forward, try to block the ball with the body and/or field the ball off the nonglove foot. Occasionally a ground ball may bounce high, in which case the ball is taken about head high. Use two hands to field the ball if possible. Concentration, alertness, and quickness are essential to good fielding of ground balls.

Thrown Balls

The same ready position is assumed for catching *thrown balls* as is used for grounders or fly balls. However, the position should not be assumed until the last moment before the ball is to be caught. This avoids warning the approaching base runners of the closeness of the play. (See figures 4.12 and 4.13.)

First, wait for the ball in a position of readiness with the feet comfortably spread, weight evenly distributed on the balls of the feet and on the hips, with knees slightly bent. Never take your eyes off the ball. If the ball comes to you below your waist, put your little fingers together and point the fingers downward; if it comes to you above your waist, put the thumbs together and point your fingers upward (see figure 4.14). This hand action permits better arm freedom and

a   b

Figure 4.13
Covering base. (a) Springing off base;
(b) releasing ball.

below waist   **above waist**

Figure 4.14
Catching position.

eliminates the possibility of the ball jamming the ends of your fingers. Next, as the ball enters the mitt or glove, allow your hands to retreat toward your body. This action is called "giving" and deadens the speed of the ball so that it is less likely to bound out of the glove. Simultaneously with the "give," cover the ball with your throwing hand so that the ball is trapped inside the glove. Immediately begin to grip the ball for the throw.

A common accident among inexperienced softball players is a jammed finger when trying to catch a ball. How can a player prevent this?

FIELDING PROBLEMS AND CORRECTIONS

Problem	Causes	Corrections
Misjudging the ball	Not paying attention	Concentrate. Talk it up.
	The wind	Check wind direction and strength.
	Slow jump on ball	Move in the direction that the ball is pitched.
Late arriving	Not ready	Assume a ready stance.
	Poor start	Keep balanced.
Fumbling	Thinking about throwing	Concentrate first on catching the ball.
Bad hop on ball	Rough infield	Smooth out.
Dropping throws or flies	Not "giving"	Relax hands as ball reaches glove.

Catch . . . touch base . . . throw

Figure 4.15
Covering a base.

Covering the Base

Wait for a throw with your feet off to the side of the base so that they will not be stepped on. If the catch is a force-out play, catch the ball, touch the base, and move immediately out of the way so that you are free to make another throw and are safe from being bumped by the runner (see figure 4.15). As the throw is made, decide where the ball will come. If the ball comes directly to the base, the baseman should move to the side of the base where the ball is coming. Place one foot on the base and stretch out to meet the throw with glove hand and glove-side foot.

Figure 4.16
Tag at a base.

Figure 4.17
Tag for the upright runner.

Figure 4.18
Fielding and throwing.

Tag Play

If the play is a tag play away from the base, make the tag and move away. The runner may be tagged with the ball in the glove. Avoid tagging a runner with the ball in your bare hand, where it can easily be jarred loose. For a tag play at a base, straddle the bag and place your glove hand in front of the base, and let the runner slide into it (see figure 4.16). If the runner comes to the base in an upright position, move to the side of the base and reach with the ball in your gloved hand to tag the runner's forward foot (see figure 4.17).

A fielder must be alert and ready to judge the ball accurately and quickly, to run rapidly and catch the ball surely, and to execute the throw immediately. Fielders must watch the ball until it is firmly resting inside their glove (see figure 4.18).

Safety

Keep several things in mind when playing defense to protect against injury.

1. When waiting for a throw, keep your feet on the side of the base so they will not be stepped on.
2. Keep your throwing hand protected behind the glove or mitt.
3. When forcing out a base runner, touch the base with your foot and move quickly away to avoid a collision.
4. When fielding a fly ball or grounder where it is possible for more than one fielder to reach it, the player in the best position should call out his or her intentions.
5. Protect your throwing hand by fielding only with the glove hand.

Practice

Individual

Grounders Stand several feet from a wall and throw the ball against it so that it will rebound off the wall to the floor or ground. Stop it in proper fielding position.

Fly Balls or Pop-ups The ability to judge and catch pop-ups or fly balls can be improved by throwing a ball as high in the air as possible and then trying to catch it.

Group

Grounders Throw or bat a grounder to each baseman, beginning with the third baseman, then the shortstop, and so on. Each fielder throws the ball to the first baseman, who throws it to the catcher. The catcher throws the ball back to first base, and the ball is then thrown to different basemen covering the bases.

Fly Balls Throw or bat fly balls to each outfielder who then throws the ball on one bounce to the catcher or to a cutoff fielder, who relays the throw on command.

Catching Fly Balls Work in pairs. Have one teammate or coach throw or bat fly balls. Practice catching fly balls that are hit (a) directly to you, (b) several feet over your head, (c) several feet in front of you, and (d) several feet diagonally forward, sideways, and backward to the right and then to the left. Work for three out of three tries before changing directions.

Reaction Footwork Drill While facing a leader, the fielders move to positions on the field. On command they move forward, sideways, and backward, utilizing proper pivoting and body positions for fielding.

DIRECTIONS FOR THE DOER:

Ask someone to check whether you are following the suggestions below while you field five ground balls, either hit or rolled directly to you from a distance of about eighty to ninety feet:

________________ Knees bent when picking up the ball.

________________ Eyes on the ball.

________________ Glove foot in front of nonglove foot about shoulder-width apart.

________________ Ball fielded off the glove foot side.

________________ Ball secured by the throwing hand.

OBSERVER:

Look at the points above. Watch the performer field five ground balls. Check the suggestions above that were followed.

Figure 4.19
Fielding checklist.

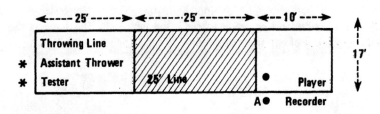

Figure 4.20
Grounder test.

Evaluation

Fielding success may be evaluated by keeping a record of your fielding average. It is computed by dividing your total putouts and assists by your total putouts, assists, and errors. A fielding average of .970 or better is considered excellent. Fielding form may be evaluated using a checklist (see figure 4.19).

Fielding Grounders Test[1]

Use dimensions listed in figure 4.20.

Testee fields twenty grounders thrown by the tester every five seconds into the shaded area. Each throw must strike the ground before passing line A. The testee fields the ball cleanly, tosses it aside, and immediately attempts to field the next throw. Score one point for each successful pickup.

1. David K. Brace, *Skills Test Manual: Softball for Girls and Softball for Boys* (Washington, D.C.: American Association for Health, Physical Education and Recreation, 1966), pp. 30–31.

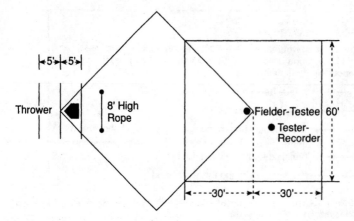

Figure 4.21
Fly ball test.

Fly Ball Test[2]

The fielder-testee stands near second base in a sixty-foot catching zone. The thrower must throw the ball over an eight-foot high rope. The fielder-testee must catch the ball, toss it aside, and be ready to catch the next ball. The score is the number of balls caught out of two trials of ten throws each. (See figure 4.21.)

Throwing

Instructional Objectives

You will be able to—

1. throw the ball with sufficient distance and accuracy for your desired defensive position,
2. throw the ball sidearm, if an infielder; overhand, if an outfielder; or with an overhand snap, if a catcher, and
3. make cutoff throws.

A good portion of defensive skill depends on the ability of the fielder to throw rapidly and accurately. No matter how well you can field a ball, if you cannot throw it properly, the value of your fielding will be considerably reduced.

The Grip

The ball should be gripped in one of two ways. The method you select should suit the size of your hand. If your hands are large, hold the ball between your thumb and first two fingers, with your third and fourth fingers resting against the ball as far around the bottom of the ball as you can comfortably reach. If your hands are

2. Ibid, pp. 32–33.

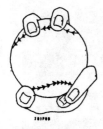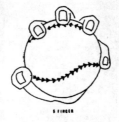

Figure 4.22
Throwing grips.

small, modify the grip so that the third and fourth fingers are spread around the side and bottom of the ball to provide better support. If possible, the fingers should cross the seams of the ball to prevent slipping when the ball is released. Only the finger pads should touch the ball. The finger pads have the best ability to feel the ball and allow maximum joint action for whipping the throw. Do not allow any other part of the hand or palm to touch it. You should be able to see daylight between your hand and the ball. Grip the ball firmly while it is still in your glove so you can quickly and surely remove it. The glove helps to support the ball as you position your fingers. (See figure 4.22.)

Basic Throws

There are five basic types of throws: the overhand, the overhand snap, the sidearm, the underhand toss, and the underhand pitch.

Throwing technique is basic to all throws. The major difference lies in the position of the hand and of the upper and lower arm in the forward thrust of the arm in the throw.

Overhand Throw

Only the arm position on the windup, or backswing, and the follow-through vary with the various types of throws. The basic throw for all players, and the only throw used by outfielders, is the overhand throw. The advantage of the overhand throw is the speed and power that can be imparted to it. The disadvantage of the overhand throw is the extra time it takes. In using the overhand throw, raise the upper arm shoulder high, lift the forearm above the head, and flex the wrist so that your hand points behind you. Lift your upper arm overhead as you move the arm forward. Make your follow-through downward. These are the steps to follow to make a good overhand throw:

1. Grip the ball firmly in the glove.
2. Shift weight backward to nonglove-side foot as you bring your nonglove hand backward.
3. Cock the wrist as you momentarily point nonglove-side elbow backward while it is shoulder high.

Figure 4.23
Throwing action.

4. Move glove-side foot forward and rotate your hips toward the target as the nonglove-side elbow comes forward near the head and the weight shifts to the forward foot.
5. Release the ball with a wrist snap as it passes the head.
6. Continue to let the body and arm follow through freely and naturally.

A maximum backward stretch will develop power for your throw. The whipping action begins in the shoulder. When you release the ball, you will be off balance unless you let your rear leg move forward to about shoulder distance from your supporting leg. If you stop the follow-through, you will lose power and accuracy.

For a long throw from the outfield, the ball is released a bit sooner than in the basic release in order to send it in a higher trajectory. The shorter the throw, the later it is released. If the throw is for a force-out play, aim it shoulder high at the receiver. If the throw is for a tag-out, it should be aimed at the base. If you must make a long throw, such as from the outfield to home plate, you can eliminate throwing the ball too high by planning to throw the ball so that it will land about ten feet in front of the receiver. The ball can then be caught on one bounce. (See figure 4.23.)

Figure 4.24
Overhand snap.

What is your point of aim on a throw for a tag-out? for a force-out? for a long throw to home plate?

The throwing arm can easily be injured. It is advisable to warm up your arm before attempting difficult throws. Throw the ball on the side of the base away from an oncoming base runner to protect the receiver of the throw.

Overhand Snap

The overhand snap throw is used primarily by the catcher and occasionally by infielders when they don't have time for a full windup. The overhand snap is executed similarly to the overhand throw, except that the windup and follow-through are shortened to save time. The windup ends when the ball is brought about to the ear. A powerful wrist snap is important to gain the distance needed. The follow-through ends almost immediately after the ball is released. (See figure 4.24.)

Underhand Toss

The underhand toss is used on short throws that must be made quickly. The upper arm and forearm are both extended down in the backswing. The wrist extends so that the hand is pointing upward. On the forward swing, the arm comes forward with the upper arm extending downward; but as the ball is released, the upper arm extends forward. If you need to cover considerable distance, whip the forearm and wrist forcefully forward. The follow-through should be up and overhead.

Sidearm Throw

The sidearm throw is most often used by infielders to throw the ball when they are in a hurry. It is executed by extending the upper arm diagonally out and down from the shoulder and extending the forearm directly up from the elbow. As the arm is

Figure 4.25
Sidearm.

Figure 4.26
Underhand pitch.

brought forward, the upper arm maintains its relative position, but the forearm is dropped down so that it is parallel with the ground. When the ball is released, the arm continues around the body sideways. (See figure 4.25.)

Underhand Pitch

The underhand pitch is used to deliver the ball to the batter (see figure 4.26). The details of proper pitching technique are discussed in chapter 5.

Advanced Defensive Skills

The Preplan

Every defensive player should be thoroughly acquainted with the ability of the batter, the placement of the base runners, the placement of the defense, the score, the number of outs, and the count on the batter. Develop a plan of action for all the various possibilities for a play in your area. As the ball is pitched, be ready to move and be convinced that the play will be in your area. Never hesitate. Hesitation time can make the difference between an out and a hit.

Cutoff Throws

The purpose of a cutoff throw is to put out an advancing runner but at the last second to allow for changing the play if the throw promises to be unsuccessful. The intervening fielder places him- or herself in line with the throw and redirects it or allows it to continue to its original destination. The decision to let the throw go

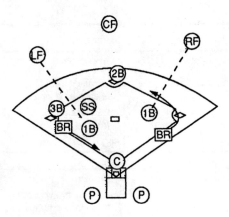

Figure 4.27
Cutoff throw.

through or to cut it off is made with the help of a nearby noninvolved teammate who can assess the possible success of the throw. The fielder must throw the ball on a line so that it is not too high for the intervening field to catch.

It is desirable for the team to predesignate the caller for cutoff throws. Usually, catchers are in the best position to call out "come through" or "cutoff." Cut off on throws from right field to home plate are most often made by the first baseman, from the left field by the shortstop, and from center field by the second baseman. Although the pitcher may cut off, he or she most often is used to back up the initial intended play. There are varying opinions concerning who should take the cutoff throw. (See figure 4.27.)

What is the purpose of a cutoff throw, and when should the intervening fielder catch a cutoff throw?

Safety

Follow these procedures against injury.

1. Warm up your arm before attempting difficult throws.
2. Throw the ball to the baseman on the side opposite from where the base runner is expected.
3. The infielder should bend down to avoid being struck by a thrown ball intended for a player beyond him.

Practice

Individual

Throw against a Wall Throw a ball against a target on the wall. The ball will rebound, and if you stand close enough, you will be able to catch it on the rebound (see figure 4.28).

Problem	Causes	Corrections
Ball Misses Target		
Right or high	Releasing ball too soon	Snap wrist. Hold off the release a bit longer.
	Off balance	Stress shifting weight forward and pivot.
Left or low	Releasing too late	Let go of ball sooner.
Ball Is Short of Target	Weak throwing arm	Change to less demanding position.
		Strengthen throwing arm through weight training.

Figure 4.28
Throwing practice.

Throwing to Bases Throwing to bases can be practiced by standing near a corner of a large room and throwing the ball against one wall, catching it and throwing it at the wall to your right or left.

Throwing from the Outfield Stand in outfield position with several balls. Place a target in the infield, such as a tire or a cone, and attempt to hit it.

Throwing for Distance After warming up your arm by practice throwing, progressively increase the distance that the ball can be thrown. Mark that distance. During each practice attempt to exceed that distance.

Group

Back and Forth Work in pairs, facing each other. The receiver sets a target for the thrower. Winner is first player to reach twenty.

Throwing Evaluation

Name _____ Date _____

Key: 5 = Excellent; 4 = Very Good; 3 = Average; 2 = Fair; 1 = Poor

Item	Rating	Comments
1. Grip	5 4 3 2 1	
2. Backward motion	5 4 3 2 1	
3. Forward motion	5 4 3 2 1	
4. Wrist snap	5 4 3 2 1	
5. Follow-through	5 4 3 2 1	

Figure 4.29
Throwing evaluation.

Three in a Line Work in threes in a straight line. The end player with the ball throws it to the target set by the middle player who pivots after catching the ball and throws it to the opposite end player's target. Repeat going backward. Score for successful target throws may be kept. Repeat practices suggested for fielding, except stress the quality of the throw.

Evaluation

Several reliable and valid skills tests for throwing are described in physical education measurement and evaluation texts. Accuracy and distance are the variables most often measured.

Throw for Distance

From a six-foot approach area, take three tries at throwing for distance. Measure the best throw to the nearest foot.

Repeated Throwing

Throw the ball repeatedly against a wall from behind a line fifteen feet from the wall. The ball must hit above a seven-and-a-half-foot line. The score is the number of hits against the wall in thirty seconds. The best of six tries is counted.

The correct technique when performing softball skills may be evaluated by using a criterion checklist. Figure 4.29 is a sample of such a checklist for evaluating throwing.

Defensive Position Play

5

Fielding and catching are the fundamental defensive measures. The defensive team prevents runs from scoring by using these skills; however, each position requires its special application. All softball players should understand the basic requirements of each position in order to work together as a team.

The Pitcher

Instructional Objectives

You will be able to—

1. pitch with accuracy in fast- or slow-pitch softball and with considerable speed in fast-pitch softball to deter successful hitting, and
2. field the ball and throw out the batter or other base runners.

The pitcher is crucial to success in fast-pitch softball. The initiation of activity begins with the pitcher, and probably 75 percent of winning in fast-pitch softball will depend on pitching. Strength and stamina are important attributes for a pitcher. In addition, excellent physique, energy, alertness, wisdom, and courage are needed. The most important requirement in either fast- or slow-pitch play, however, is accuracy or control. The pitcher must have the ability to pitch the ball consistently over the plate and in the strike zone. In fast-pitch softball, the objective is to make it impossible for the batter to hit the ball. Thus, speed and deception are needed on each pitch. In slow-pitch softball, however, only accuracy is required, since the objective is to get the batter out after he or she has hit the ball.

Fast-Pitch Pitching

Concentrated practice is necessary to develop and control the variety of pitches necessary. Most fast-pitch pitchers use a windmill or a slingshot type of delivery. Windups have two purposes: (1) to deceive the batter and (2) to obtain full power from your entire body to add force to the pitch. Develop the windup and delivery that suits you best. There is a variety of pitches: fastball, change of pace, drop, curves, and a rise, or upshoot, pitch. Start your pitch by standing with your pivot foot, which is your glove-side foot, on the pitcher's plate and the nonpivot foot on or behind the pitcher's plate. Both feet must be on the ground within the twenty-four-inch length of the pitcher's plate. Face the batter; your shoulders must be in line with first and third bases, and the ball shall be held in one hand. Your feet

Figure 5.1
Fast-pitch foot position.

should be approximately twelve inches apart. Only from this position can you take the signal from the catcher. After assuming this "ready" position you may hold the ball in both hands for not less than one second or more than ten seconds before releasing it toward the batter.

Fast-pitch pitching rules vary for men and women in regard to the feet position on the pitching plate and the step forward as the ball is delivered. Men must keep their pivot foot in contact with the pitching plate and the nonpivot foot on or behind the plate. As they step forward to deliver the ball, both feet may be in the air at the same time. Women must keep both feet on contact with the pitcher's plate, and their pivot foot must remain in contact or push off and drag away from the pitching plate prior to the front foot touching the ground. (See figure 5.1.)

Deliveries

The ball is delivered to the plate in predominantly three ways: the windmill, slingshot, and the straight pitch. (See figure 5.2.)

Windmill

The *windmill delivery* makes a complete circle from straight up overhead to behind your body and then downward and out toward the batter. It is used by most advanced-level pitchers in fast-pitch softball because it generates the most momentum for speed. Start the delivery with both arms moving forward and upward, reaching out without stretching. Shift your weight to the foot on the pitching-arm side. As you take the ball from the glove, extend the upper arm diagonally outward from the shoulder and the forearm diagonally inward toward the body. As the hand reaches head high, begin to lift the opposite foot off the rubber and forward in order to keep your balance. The arm is completely extended when it is dropped behind the body from head high. You will gain momentum as you move into your downward swing. The nonpivot foot completes its step toward the plate to brace your

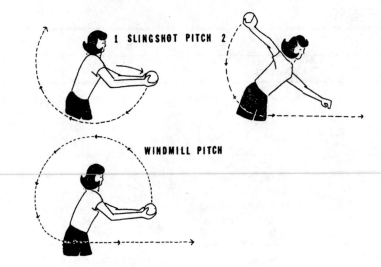

Figure 5.2
Pitching windups.

body for the forward action and release of the ball. The pitching arm is thrust forward by pushing with the pivot foot against the rubber and then transferring this weight forward. Start the forward motion with your body rotating forward, the arm swung downward and forward, parallel with the lateral line of the body. Bring your body weight forward as you take a natural step toward the batter on the foot opposite the pitching arm. When the extended arm is about even with the side of the body just before the ball is released, snap your wrist forward and roll the ball off your fingertips to add power and spin to the pitch. After the ball leaves your hand, the arm continues to follow through, up and overhead with the arm completely extended.

Slingshot

The *slingshot* usually provides more control but with slightly less speed and it is more often used in less advanced play. Start your backswing by moving both hands forward toward the batter until your arms are comfortably extended straight out in front about waist high. When this point is reached, bring your throwing arm down and back along the hip line and up behind the body as far as it can comfortably extend. At the top of the backswing, cock your wrist by extending as far back as possible. The upper arm and forearm are diagonally upward, and the body is rotated almost a quarter turn toward the pitching-arm side. Your follow-through is similar to the windmill delivery. The foot on the pitching-arm side is brought up next to the forward foot in a fairly wide stance with the knees and hips relaxed. This position permits maximum balance after release of the ball and also puts you in a ready fielding position. (See figure 5.3.)

Action	Fast Pitch	Slow Pitch
Delivery	Underhand	Same
Feet	Males: The pivot foot must be in contact with pitching plate and the nonpivot foot on or behind plate. Females: Both feet in contact with pitcher's plate. All: Both feet on ground within 24″ of pitcher's plate.	Only one foot must be on the plate.
Step	One step may be taken toward the batter as ball is delivered. Males: Both feet can be in the air at the same time. Females: Pivot foot must remain in contact or push off and drag away from pitching plate prior to the front foot touching the ground.	Pivot foot must be in contact with pitching plate through delivery.
Speed	Any amount permitted	Moderate speed with a perceptible arc, not over 12 feet
Strike Zone	Over the plate and between batter's armpits and the tops of his or her knees	Over the plate and no higher than the batter's shoulders or lower than his or her knees
Windup	Only one motion toward the batter is legal.	Same except in 16-inch play, where two hesitations are permitted

Figure 5.3
Slingshot pitch.

Straight Pitch

The *straight pitch* is a control pitch and is similar to the slingshot but the back-swing is less. It is most often used in slow-pitch softball. The forward motion, release, and follow-through are similar to the other deliveries.

As you develop your speed and control, try to release your fast pitch so that it will "break" by curving, rising, or dropping. Do not attempt to toss or pull the arm, but rather swing the arm freely and powerfully on your delivery.

Note that the difference between the windmill and slingshot deliveries is in the initial action of the pitching arm; that is up, over, down, and forward for the windmill, and back, up, down, and forward for the slingshot delivery.

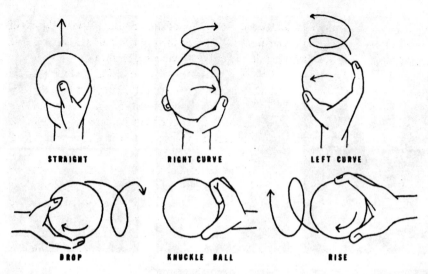

Figure 5.4
Pitching grips and releases.

Regardless of which delivery you use, the following elements are important to your pitching motion:

1. Cock the wrists on the backswing and snap them on the release.
2. Maintain balance on the forward swing by lifting the nonpivot foot as you stride forward.
3. Brush the hip at the point of release.
4. Develop a consistent stride.
5. Drive off the rubber with the nonpivot foot for power.

Types of Pitches

Once you have developed control and speed, you should learn other types of pitches (see figure 5.4). These pitches cause the ball to drop, to curve, to rise, and to change speeds in order to make it more difficult for the batter to hit the ball. Regardless of the type of pitch, the pitching action should be similar so that the batter does not know what kind of a pitch to expect.

For the *straight fast pitch* and the *slingshot delivery,* grip the ball as for any other throw except that the hand is under the ball. Again, as for other throws, use either your entire hand or the tripod grip. Be sure your finger pads cross the seams of the ball.

A *curveball* makes the ball spin either toward or away from the batter. To pitch a curveball, grip the ball as for the fastball, but as it is released, snap the wrist to the left or to the right to cause the ball to roll off the inside or outside of the hand. The direction of the snap depends on the direction you wish the ball to curve. Snap the wrist to the left to make the ball curve left and to the right to make it curve right. The *drop* makes the ball curve or break sharply downward. Use the same grip and delivery as for the fastball, but at the instant of the release, lift your thumb off the ball first, and then snap your first two fingers sharply upward. This action gives the ball more forward spin so that it will curve downward, or drop.

The grip for the *rise* or *upshoot pitch* differs in that the ball is held with the fingers on top of the ball with the thumb underneath. As you release the ball, the wrist is extended or snapped upward, and the thumb pushes forward against the ball. This action imparts a backspin that should make the ball rise as it nears home plate. The effectiveness of these pitches will increase as you learn to add speed to the pitch. The *change-of-pace pitch* or *change-up pitch* slows down the pitch and tends to throw off the timing of the batter. There are many grips for the change-of-pace pitch. The ball may be held in the palm of the hand with the fingers held loosely on the ball. It may be held by the knuckles or by digging your fingernails into it. Your pitching motion is again the same, but at the release the hand is opened with a snap of all four fingers, and the thumb merely extends forward. The ball must be released with equal pressure all around the ball so that no spin is imparted to it. The absence of spin will cause the ball to float or sail toward the batter. Controlling these various pitches and the development of speed will give you what is called "stuff." Concentrate first on pitching with as much speed and spin as you can accurately control.

What is the effect on a pitched ball of a wrist snap to the left on the release?

Slow-Pitch Pitching

Since the ball must travel through an arc of at least six feet and no more than twelve feet, many pitchers will try to control the ball so that it reaches the maximum height close to the batter. The ball will descend as it crosses the plate and will be even with his or her back shoulder. This type of pitch often results in a pop-up. The slow-pitch pitcher should try to pitch to the desired corners of the plate and vary the height of the arc of the pitched ball. It is legal and desirable to place spins on the ball: forward, backward, or sideward.

Since only one foot must be in contact with the pitching plate (figure 5.5), be sure that the supporting foot is on the front edge of the plate so that when your stride is taken, your body can be as close to the target as possible at the instant of release.

How should the ball be gripped and released to deliver the upshoot pitch?

Defensive Responsibilities

Pitchers have many defensive responsibilities. You must be able to field bunts, check runners on base, cover bases, and back up throws.

Covering

Whenever the catcher leaves the plate and a runner can score, you must cover the plate. Don't block the plate. Give the runner the outside of the plate and tag with the ball in the glove.

a   b

Figure 5.5
Slow pitch. (a) Start; (b) forward step.

Backing

Usually the pitcher will back up third base. Move twenty feet behind the base on a hit to the outfield when a play is anticipated.

Cutoff Plays

Move approximately twenty feet in front of the plate to the side that the throw is expected. Raise both arms overhead. The catcher will call for the cutoff and where to throw the ball. If no directions are given, allow the ball to go through to the catcher.

Defensive Responsibilities—Fast-Pitch Only

After a Pitch Receive the ball from the catcher in front of the rubber. If there is a base runner, check the runner back and be sure you are in the pitcher's circle. Walk behind the pitcher's rubber while facing second base. Turn toward the batter and assume the correct pitching position. Envision a strike on every pitch.

Bunts In advanced play, most bunts are fielded by the first and third basemen because they move in very close to the plate. However, particular defense will necessitate your fielding bunts. Use the fielding techniques described for infielders.

Problem	Causes	Corrections
Ball too high or far from batter	Release too late or stride too short	Release sooner. Practice consistent striding by marking desired spot.
Ball too low or close to batter	Release too soon or stride too long	Release later. Practice consistent stride.
Insufficient speed	Incorrect delivery action	Increase leverage by rotating spine and hip on throwing side away from batter. Stride as arm moves forward. Move arm forward as fast as possible. Snap the wrist on release.
Loss of balance	Incorrect stride and weight shift	Practice stride. Bring pitching-side foot up parallel with supporting foot after release of the ball.
	Incorrect stance	Feet shoulder-width apart

Safety

Pitching is demanding, and it can be a dangerous position.

1. Be alert and balanced after delivering the ball to avoid being hit by sharply batted balls.
2. Be sure that the pitching plate and soil around the pitching area are firm to prevent slipping.

Practice

Individual

Mimetic Pitching For about ten minutes daily, practice your pitching form without using a ball. Assume stance, concentration, and take your windup, delivery, and follow-through.

Target Practice Construct the strike zone on the wall or a piece of carpet hung in front of a wall. Take a basket of balls and pitch to planned areas on the target.

Speed Increase speed as accuracy develops. Both should be practiced together. Try to pitch as fast as possible with accuracy.

Leg Strength Run several times around the field daily to increase leg strength and overall physical endurance.

Group

Batting Practice Pitch batting practice as a means of becoming accustomed to the individual batter's position and relation to the strike zone.

Observed Practice Have someone with a checklist of the essential pitching fundamentals check out adherence to form.

Evaluation

Win-Loss Record

Compile the total wins and losses.

Earned Run Record

Compute the Earned Run Average (ERA) by adding all earned runs scored against the pitcher as a result of base runners getting on base other than by errors and by adding all the innings pitched. Multiply the earned runs by seven and divide by the innings pitched. The formula is

$$\frac{\text{ER (earned runs)} \times 7 \text{ (innings in a game)}}{\text{IP (total innings pitched)}}$$

Accuracy Test

Place a target on the wall as per figure 5.6. Fifteen legal pitches are permitted. Pitched balls striking within or on the line marking the inner rectangle count two points. Balls hitting the outer rectangle count one point. The score is the sum of points made.

How should the pitcher prepare for a cutoff play?

The Catcher

Instructional Objectives

You will be able to—

1. catch the balls thrown by the pitcher,
2. give reliable and accurate targets for the pitcher,
3. decide the pitch needed and signal the pitcher,
4. field the ball and throw out base runners, and
5. direct the infield on where the play should be made on a bunt.

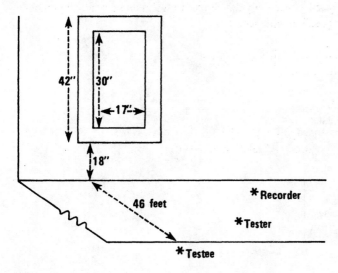

Figure 5.6
Accuracy test.

The catcher is an important defensive position in fast-pitch softball, since base runners can steal bases and advance on wild pitches and passed balls. In slow pitch, the catcher may be one of the weakest fielding players because of the following differences:

1. bunting or stealing is not allowed,
2. the ball is dead after each called ball or strike, and
3. the slow arching pitch is not as dangerous as a fast straight pitch.

The catcher is the sparkplug of the team. This player not only catches the pitches but also is in the best position to direct team defensive play. The catcher should be agile, alert, strong in the legs, and able to react quickly and should be a natural leader with a competitive spirit and the ability to think quickly, decisively, and logically. A strong throwing arm is essential. The catcher is responsible for giving the pitcher advice on the type of pitch and the target for the pitch, catching pop-ups, throwing out runners attempting to steal, fielding bunts, protecting home plate, and backing up play at first or third base.

Since the catcher faces the entire defense, he or she serves as the defensive leader. The catcher calls out who is to field bunts, pop-ups, and short fly balls. Team spirit and hustle are encouraged and maintained by the catcher's example. If the pitcher gets upset, develops some pitching flaw, or begins to pitch too fast, the catcher should walk out to the pitcher to talk, encourage, and in general try to settle the pitcher down. The rules require that the catcher be in the catcher's box to receive the pitch, not interfere with the batter's attempt to swing at the ball, and wear a mask to protect the face.

Target—Fast Pitch

After the signal is accepted, give the pitcher the target for the pitch by holding your mitt at the desired spot. As you hold your mitt up for the target clench the throwing

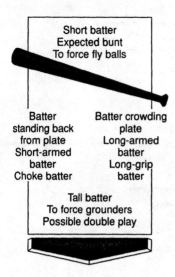

Figure 5.7
Pitching area for strike zones.

hand in a loose fist to protect the fingers from the ball. Continue to hold the mitt on the target as the pitcher starts to pitch. When the ball leaves the pitcher's hand, move up to a semistanding position with your feet spread diagonally outward approximately three feet apart. The change of position allows greater freedom of movement to catch the ball, to field it, or to throw out a runner. If the pitch should come low into the dirt, drop your left leg down parallel with the ground to block the ball. When the ball reaches your glove or mitt, absorb the force of the pitch by "relaxing" your arms into your waist.

Avoid giving a target in the middle of the strike zone. Keep the target steady until the ball leaves the pitcher's hand. The pitcher and catcher should study the batter and organize a strategy. The pitcher should throw balls that the batter finds difficult to hit. The ball should be pitched over the inside corner of the plate to batters who stand close to the plate, and over the outside corner of the plate to batters who stand far away from the plate. If the batter crouches, pitch the ball high. If the batter stands erect, pitch low balls. Change the pace of your delivery to power hitters and pitch fastballs to weak hitters. If the batter strides toward the pitch as he/she swings, pitch the ball inside. If the stride is away, aim your pitch to the outside corner of the plate. When the batter takes a long stride into the pitch, pitch high balls; conversely, if the batter takes a short stride, pitch low balls. (See figure 5.7.)

If a weak batter stands erect and away from the plate, what kind of pitch is recommended?

The catcher must adjust his or her target and the type of pitch when there are base runners. With less than two outs and runners on base, the pitcher should pitch low and inside to force the batter to hit the ball into the ground for a double play

Figure 5.8
Catcher stand-up stance.

Figure 5.9
Catcher sit-down stance.

or to prevent the batter from hitting the ball behind the runner on a hit-and-run play. If a bunt is expected, the pitch should be kept high, because these pitches are often popped up.

Pitching patterns depend on the pitcher's control. Every pitcher must aim at a target, however, and the target should be a most effective one for that batter at that particular time and in that particular situation.

Stance—Fast Pitch

The signal and the target for the pitch are given by the catcher when in a squat position. The squat position is assumed by bending the hips, knees, and ankles so that the body is as low as possible without resting the buttock on the ankles or the ground. Weight is on the toes, and knees are comfortably spread outward. At this point, fast-pitch catchers choose one of two stances. Some "stand up," whereas others continue to "sit down," as illustrated in figures 5.8 and 5.9. The sit-down catcher stays on his or her haunches for the target. As the ball is pitched, the catcher rises on his or her toes into a crouch and thus is ready to meet the pitch, pivot, throw, or field. The stand-up catcher's stance is a bit more popular. Stand with knees bent and legs wide apart with the left foot ahead of the right. If the catcher is tall, this position is awkward and requires a great deal of bending. In general, the catcher's stance often depends on the catcher's preference, ability, type of pitch, and the baserunning situation.

Figure 5.10
Slow-pitch stance.

Stance—Slow Pitch

The slow-pitch catching stance usually begins about one-half a bat length farther away from the plate than the fast-pitch stance. Since the ball is arching downward, the glove or mitt is held out for the target but then lowered about shin high to catch the ball before or after it bounces. (See figure 5.10.)

Signals

The catcher and pitcher should agree on signals for the pitch. The catcher gives signals by extending the fingers of the throwing hand against the inside of his or her thigh when down in a squat position. Effort must be made to hide the signal from the offensive team. Hiding the signals is enhanced by placing the mitt slightly in front of the knees.

Throwing

The preparation for throwing must be accomplished quickly. The catcher uses a snap throw to the pitcher and, if strong enough, a snap throw to throw out runners attempting to steal and to field a bunt. With runners on base, the catcher should constantly try to reduce their leadoff by walking out in front of the plate and threatening to throw to the base or by simply walking them back to base. An occasional snap throw to the base may catch a base runner too far off to get back safely.

A snap throw begins from behind the ear and is thrown overhand with a snap of the wrist. The feet must be shuffled from the squat or stand-up stance so that the nonthrowing-side hip and foot are moving toward the intended target. Do not straighten up completely or move in front of the plate. The throw should be free of spin and aimed at the fielder's knees on the side of the anticipated play. Do not wait for the infielder to cover the base.

Fielding Responsibilities

Catchers must catch pop flies, field bunts, retrieve passed balls and wild pitches, back up first base, cover home plate, pick off runners, and often direct cutoff throws. Immediately flip off the mask when you must assume a fielding responsibility.

Catching Pop Flies

Infielders should be allowed to catch pop flies if they can easily reach them. If the ball is behind you, you should turn your back to the infield and run for it. Catch the ball over your head with both hands.

The Bunt

Move with the batter, stay low, pick up the ball with your throwing hand. If the ball is toward first base, field the ball with the dominant foot forward to avoid any extra step. If the ball is down the third base side, run in a semicircle so the ball is picked up while facing first base.

Retrieving Wild Passed and Pitched Balls

No retrieval is necessary if no runners are on base. Move immediately to retrieve the ball if there are base runners, field it, and immediately turn to deter the runner from advancing or to attempt a putout.

Backing Up First Base

If no runners are in potential scoring positions, the catcher should back up all throws to first base. Move diagonally away from the base line and toward first base as soon as a ground ball is hit.

Covering Home Plate

Await the throw in front of home plate, show the base runner only a small part of the outside corner of the plate, catch the ball, turn outside, and tag the runner. If the runner is sliding, drop your right knee, turn left, and put the glove low and let the runner slide into it. Blocking the plate is dangerous but is often done in advanced play. (See figure 5.11.)

a b

Figure 5.11
Covering home plate. (a) Tagging; (b) blocking.

Picking Off

The rules for fast pitch permit base stealing and leading off after the ball leaves the pitcher's hand. When playing sixteen-inch slow-pitch softball, the base runners may lead off at any time. In all types of play, the base runner may not leave the base until the pitched ball is batted, hits the ground, or passes home plate. Therefore, in fast-pitch play and sixteen-inch slow-pitch play, the catcher must be alert to picking off base runners if they stray too far from the base.

Cutoff Plays

You are usually responsible for calling the play for a cutoff. Call "cut" and identify the base to which the ball is to be thrown. Give no directions if the ball is to continue on course.

Infielders

Instructional Objectives

You will be able to—

1. know how to play the various defensive positions,
2. catch balls thrown by teammates to put out base runners,
3. field batted and thrown balls, and
4. cover the back up assigned bases.

Playing the infield requires specific physical ability and skill for each position. However, all infielders, including the pitcher and the catcher, must constantly be

Position of Base Runners?
Outs?
Count?

Figure 5.12
Awareness needed.

Figure 5.13
First baseman put-out position.

aware of the immediate situation such as (1) number of outs, (2) count on the batter, and (3) position of the base runners (see figure 5.12). With this information, you must think through what action you will need to play your position before each pitch. This process is fostered through constant communication with other infielders.

First Baseman

The first baseman is involved in almost every play. Agility and height are helpful physical attributes for this position. Throwing to other bases is easier for left-handed players. The first baseman plays about six feet toward second base and two to three steps in front of the base. In fast-pitch play and/or when bunting is legal and a bunt is expected, the first and third basemen should play one-third or halfway to the plate. The exact distance depends on the speed of the bunter.

When two strikes have been called, you can move back four or five steps, since a bunt is less likely. You receive all kinds of throws. Nimble footwork is essential. To cover the base for a putout, the first baseman stands in the usual ready position, facing the throw. If the ball comes straight to you, step toward the ball with the foot on the mitt side and touch the bag with the opposite foot. Reach for the ball to save time. (See figure 5.13.) If the ball comes wide of the mitt side, step to that side, and touch the bag with the same foot as for the straight-in throw. If the ball comes wide to the nonmitt side, reach across with the mitt to catch it and touch the base with the foot opposite the mitt side. On a pick-off play when the catcher throws the ball to try to put out the runner, if time permits, straddle the bag with your feet facing second base and rotate the upper part of your body toward the throw. When you catch the ball, swing the mitt down on the bag.

Second Baseman

The second baseman plays about fifteen feet toward first base from second base and about ten feet behind the baseline. Your job is to catch any fly balls or field any grounders in this territory. Since most of the second baseman's throws will go to first base or to the shortstop covering second base, a strong throwing arm is not necessary. However, agility in covering the base and ability to throw the ball quickly aids the second baseman in making double plays. When you are the middleman for a double play at second base, you run so that you will catch the ball as

Figure 5.14
Double play with second baseman.

Figure 5.15
Force-out and relay throw.

you step on the base with your left foot. After catching the ball, you take one more step with your right foot to leave the base; then pivot on the right foot, and step forward with the left foot as you throw to first base. The second baseman must be alert to receive throws from the catcher on attempted steals and on bunt plays to cover first base. (See figures 5.14 and 5.15.)

Shortstop

This very demanding position requires agility, speed, and a good throwing arm. The shortstop plays about halfway between third and second base and about ten to twelve feet behind the baseline. As a shortstop you must be quick, agile, able to throw off balance and to run rapidly. When you are the pivot person on a double play, you usually run directly to the base, reaching it in time to receive the throw, tag the base, and get rid of the ball before the base runner can break up the play. If the throw is from the second baseman, step past the bag with the left foot, drag the

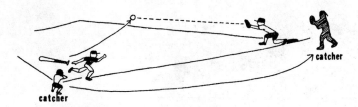

Figure 5.16
Backing up bases.

right foot across the bag and throw. If the throw is from the first baseman, the ball should come to the front side of the bag. In this situation, come to a quick stop, touch the base with the left foot, and then throw the ball.

Third Baseman

Third base is called the "hot corner" because most batters are right-handed and tend to "pull" their hits toward third base. Therefore, as a third baseman, you must be able to field and throw in a rapid, smooth sequence. The position of the third baseman in fast pitch varies according to the situation. You will be constantly changing your position. Because the bunt is so prevalent in advanced play, you will play sometimes halfway to home plate. Normally, you will play about fifteen feet from third base when a bunt is expected and about five to ten feet in front of third base when a bunt is not expected. Play close enough to the line so that a ball down the line could be reached with one stride. These distances will vary with the speed of the pitch and the side from which the batter bunts. You will field all ground balls and pop flies hit in your area and cover third base on all putout plays. In slow pitch, the third baseman may always play back because bunting is illegal.

How do fast-pitch and slow-pitch softball differ in regard to stealing bases and leading off?

Infielder Defensive Responsibilities

Infielders have a variety of duties to perform and their execution varies depending on the situation relative to the score, position of base runners, and placement of the batted ball. These duties are backing up and covering bases, cutting off throws, and tagging out runners on a trap play.

Backing Up Bases

Every defensive player has a responsibility to back up plays in his or her area. Backing up is used to prevent the taking of an additional base because of an error. The first baseman occasionally backs up home. (See figure 5.16.)

Covering

Each baseman is responsible for protecting his or her base. Be ready at all times to catch a throw to your base to put out a runner. However, occasionally you will be

Figure 5.17
Trapping a runner.

forced to field a ball while another runner is advancing to your base. In this case, the nearest available defensive player should be prepared to run to your base and take the thrown ball to put out the runner. The second baseman covers first base if the first baseman is forced to field a batted ball. In this situation, the shortstop automatically moves to second base to cover the base. If the shortstop is fielding a ball and a play is to be made to second base, the second baseman covers the base. If the third baseman is fielding the ball, the shortstop will cover third base. These covering maneuvers can often be anticipated, but when they cannot, an advanced player moves instinctively to protect the base near him or her.

Trapping a Runner

When a base runner is caught between two bases, he or she is referred to as being trapped. The play is called a rundown. In this situation defensive players close in on the runner from either side, throwing the ball to the player toward whom the runner is moving. In the meantime, other players back up the throw to protect against an overthrown ball or to tag out the runner if he or she should elude the trap. It is a good technique to fake a throw and then move toward the runner with the ball. Always chase the runner back to the base they came from. Run-down fielders should position themselves slightly to the side of the base to avoid throwing into the runner.

In the meantime, the first defensive player runs at the base runner as the second defensive player positions himself or herself inside the baseline just in front of the base. The first option is to be able to outrun the base runner and tag him or her out. If this is not possible, the ball should be thrown to the second defensive player to tag out the runner. This can only be accomplished if the base runner is forced to retreat at such speed that he or she cannot reverse directions. (See figure 5.17.)

Cutoff Plays

A cutoff is used to put out an advancing runner. The pitcher may act to intercept a thrown ball or cut it off and redirect the ball if the catcher directs such action. Occasionally, the outfielder may not be able to throw on a line from where the ball is retrieved or caught. In this situation, the closest infielder must be alert to be in position to raise his or her arms in a "U" to serve as a cutoff target. Redirect the ball as directed by the catcher. Redirecting the ball is called a *relay throw* (see figure 5.18).

Figure 5.18
Relay throw.

INFIELDING PROBLEMS AND CORRECTIONS

Problems	Causes	Corrections
Throw too late for a putout	Not charging the ball	Come to meet the ball.
	Taking too long to release the ball	Practice throwing from a semistanding position.
	Weak arm	Play a position needing less arm strength.
Failure to cover the base	Not thinking ahead	Infielders must communicate.
Failure to back up a play	Lack of concentration	Practice and reminders

Practice

Individual

Mimetic Footwork Assume ready fielding position and practice moving forward, backward, and sideways to field the ball and then to move over to the base to cover.

Pivot and Throw Place a base about ten feet from the wall. Position yourself the usual playing distance from the base. Place a ball on the floor at that point; then, pick it up, run to the base, and throw the ball against the wall.

Pop-ups Throw a ball vertically at differing heights. Practice trying to catch the ball.

Group

Infield Practice Throw or hit the ball from the batter's position to each infielder. The infielder fields the ball and throws to first base. The ball is then thrown to the catcher, catcher to third baseman, to second baseman, to first baseman, and

Defensive Evaluation		

Name _____**Position** _____

Key: 5 = Excellent, 4 = Very Good, 3 = Average, 2 = Fair, 1 = Poor

Item	Rating	Comments
1. Ready position	5 4 3 2 1	
2. Fielding position	5 4 3 2 1	
3. Throwing	5 4 3 2 1	
4. Covering	5 4 3 2 1	
5. Tagging	5 4 3 2 1	
6. Backing bases	5 4 3 2 1	

Figure 5.19
Outfielder evaluation form.

then back to the catcher. The catcher flips the ball to the hitter or thrower who repeats the action to each infielder. The initial throw after fielding the ball may be made to other bases.

Trapping the Runners Place a base runner between two infielders. The base runner attempts to return or advance to a base before being put out. Fielders practice throwing the ball and chasing the runner to make the putout. Add the various backup and covering assignments of the remaining infielders.

Double Play Place a runner on first base and a base runner at home plate. A ball is thrown or batted to an infielder, who attempts to complete the double play. (Sliding can be practiced by the runner approaching second base.)

Evaluation

Fielding Record

Keep a record of the attempted putouts and assists and the successful putouts and assists. To determine an average, divide the number by successes by the number of attempts.

$$\frac{\text{Successes}}{\text{Attempts}} = \text{Average of Fielding Success}$$

Rating Chart

Ask an observer to evaluate your fielding performance using the chart in figure 5.19.

Outfielders

Instructional Objectives

You will be able to—

1. play the various positions,
2. catch a fly ball hit into your assigned area and throw the ball to the proper infielder to force out or to contain the actions of the base runner,
3. field ground balls, and
4. make appropriate defensive plays: backing and holding a runner to their base.

An outfielder must be a good runner and possess a strong throwing arm. The distance in or out that an outfielder plays depends on several factors: the wind, the batter's ability, the score, the inning, and the location of base runners. In addition, the basic position is varied by moving to your right for left-handed hitters and to your left for right-handed hitters. The movement is increased in either direction for pull hitters.

An outfielder must learn to judge the ball immediately, run rapidly to catch the ball, and return the throw as quickly as possible. In addition to fielding the ball, outfielders back up plays at various bases in their areas, as well as for the outfielders nearest to them. Outfielders must be aware of base runners as well as the number of outs. The outfielder must decide as the ball is caught whether he or she can throw out a base runner. If a putout is possible, the outfielder will throw the ball on a line directly to the base. If the outfielder cannot throw that far on a direct line, he or she will throw the ball so that it will land a few feet in front of the base and hop into the infielder's glove. If it is not possible to gain a putout, the outfielder will return the ball one base ahead of the runner closest to home plate. Always avoid making unnecessary throws. When the ball is hit deep and the throw is too long to reach its destination on one hop, throw to the second baseman or shortstop, who will relay the throw. The glare of the sun or field lights can sometimes hamper the vision of outfielders. Outfielders wear sunglasses, burnt cork, or shield their eyes from glare. It is the outfielder's responsibility to be aware of the wind direction and velocity, as well as the usual habits of the batter, and to adjust his or her position in the outfield accordingly. Short fly balls falling between the infield and outfield are usually the responsibility of the outfielders, since it is easier to move forward than backward. Outfielders must call out their intentions on these plays. It is imperative that outfielders communicate to each other whenever the ball is hit into areas that overlap.

Center Fielder

The center fielder plays behind second base and is the fastest and most aggressive player in the outfield. As the center fielder, you are the leader of the outfield. Priority is given to you to field all balls to either the left or right. It is your responsibility to direct the proper playing positions of the other outfielders. The center fielder directs where the throw is to be made from the outfield. You will back up the other outfielders and the second baseman. When the ball is hit between two outfielders, the center fielder cuts over for the ball, and the other outfielders cut behind him to back up the play as noted in figure 5.20.

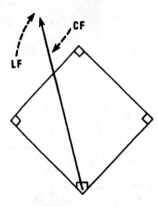

Figure 5.20
Ball hit between outfielders.

Left Fielder

The left fielder plays in the outfield between the third baseman and the shortstop, and backs up the center fielder and the third baseman when necessary. Usually the left fielder will play a bit closer to the foul line for right-handed hitters and a bit closer to center field for left-handed pull hitters. In addition, the left fielder backs up all throws made from the right side of the field.

Right Fielder

The right fielder plays between first and second base and backs up the center fielder and the first baseman when necessary. Usually the right fielder plays a bit closer to the foul line for left-handed pull hitters and closer to the center fielder for right-handed hitters. In addition the right fielder backs up all plays made from the left side of the field.

Short Fielder

The short fielder is the tenth player permitted in slow-pitch softball. This person may play as an extra infielder or outfielder or as a roving player. The exact position is determined by the team preference and/or situation. If the batter is a long-ball hit-ter, the short fielder may play as an outfielder; if the batter is an excellent place-hitter, then the short fielder may play as an extra infielder. As a rover, the short fielder plays between the infield and outfield, swinging more to the left for right-handed hitters and more to the right for left-handed hitters. The short fielder must be very versatile to be able to fulfill these roles. Speed, agility, and a good throwing arm are essential abilities (see figure 5.21).

No matter what your defensive roles, your ability to throw, to catch, to run, to judge the ball, and to think ahead will determine your true effectiveness.

What is the area of play for the short fielder when acting as a rover?

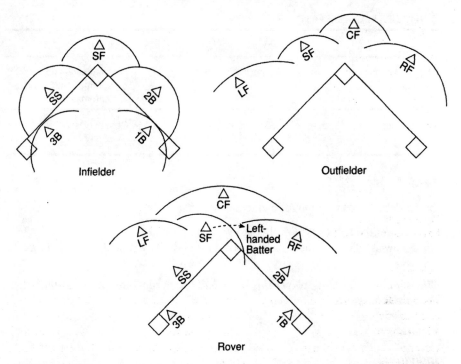

Figure 5.21
Short fielder positions (slow pitch).

Outfielder Defensive Responsibilities

Outfielders' defensive responsibilities after fielding the ball are to prevent base runners from advancing after catching a fly ball or fielding a base hit, and to back up
other outfielders and infielders nearest to them.

Backing

If the ball is not hit directly to you, move quickly to back up any adjacent outfielder
or infielder or behind the closest base to which a throw may be made. Inform the
fielder what base to throw the ball to if there are base runners.

Holding Runners

After fielding the ball, return the ball one base in advance of the lead base runner to
prevent him or her from advancing, or to a player in position to prevent the runner
from advancing.

Throwing Out Base Runners

Throw the ball hard and low to the base if a putout is possible. If a cutoff play may
be necessary, throw on a line just above the head of the cutoff player.

Problem	Causes	Corrections
Slow start on the ball	Not paying attention	Concentration and communication from teammates
Incorrect placement of throw	Poor judgment	Communication from center fielder

Safety

Outfielders should take the following precautions:

1. Call for the ball to avoid collisions with other fielders.
2. Know at all times where the fences are located. They should be padded for your protection.

Why should the fielding player throw the ball low to the base when a putout at the base is possible?

Practice

Individual

Fly Balls Throw golf balls to yourself at various angles and practice catching them.

Throwing Take a basket of softballs and practice throwing to the various bases as targets. Practice cutoff throws by placing a seven- to eight-foot marker near the infield and attempting to throw just above it.

Group

Ground Balls Ground balls are high to the various outfielders who field the ball and throw to the catcher.

Fly Balls Same as above.

Throwing to Bases All types of hits are made to the outfielders, who are directed to throw the balls to the various bases.

Evaluation

Fielding Record

Keep a record of all errors and play attempts. Divide the errors by total number of attempts. It may be useful to subdivide these totals by type of play such as catching fly balls, fielding base hits, and throwing to the base or to a cutoff player.

Patterns of Play

6

As your skill in the various softball techniques improves, so should your ability to execute these skills in planned offensive and defensive patterns. Your ability to score runs will increase when you are able to take advantage of circumstances that are conducive to getting a base hit or advancing to the next base. You should know how to adjust your position defensively to protect against offensive patterns that could result in the scoring of runs. If you are the pitcher, know the strategy as well as the techniques of pitching.

Instructional Objectives

You will be able to—

1. take advantage of prevailing defensive conditions to enhance opportunities to score runs, and
2. take advantage of prevailing offensive conditions to prevent runs from being scored.

Offensive Patterns

Batting

When batting, your foremost thought should be to get on base. This goal will be achieved most often by getting a base hit. However, an assessment of the prevailing offensive and defensive situations should guide you in deciding on any adjustments in your batting plan. Shortening your grip on the bat so that you can swing the bat faster and more accurately will help you to hit a fastball pitcher or a pitcher with a great deal of "stuff." When the pitcher seems to lack control or seems to be getting tired, try to be very selective in swinging at pitches. It is advisable not to swing at a 3–0 pitch or even a 3–1 pitch, since a walk is likely. However, if you are a power hitter, you could possibly hit a "grooved pitch" (one in the center of the strike zone) for extra bases. As the batter, you have the advantage on a 3–2 pitch since you know that the pitcher must throw the next ball in the strike zone.

Your second objective should be to advance a base runner. This can be accomplished by sacrificing, by bunting or hitting a fly ball, or by hitting the ball on the ground in the direction away from the base runner, which may force the ball to be played only on you, thus allowing the runner to advance. For example, if the runner is

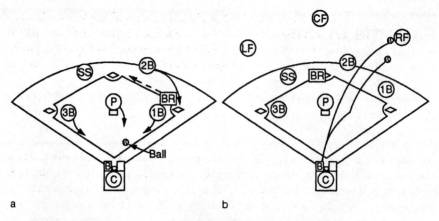

Figure 6.1

Offensive patterns. (a) Fast-pitch bunt strategy to advance base runner; (b) sacrifice hitting to advance runner.

on second base and you hit the ball to the right side of the infield, the ball most often would be played at first base to force you, allowing the runner to advance to third base. (See figure 6.1.)

Fast-Pitch Strategy

Surprise the defense with a bunt if they are playing back. Conversely, if they are playing in for a bunt, it might be wise to try to punch the ball over their heads. Swing at a pitch, but with no intention of hitting it when you know a base runner is going to steal. The swinging action confuses the catcher and often may result in a poor throw. The usual offensive pattern in a close game is to try to get a runner on base, sacrifice that player to second with a bunt, or have him or her try to steal second base so that a base hit can result in a score.

Another pattern is to score a runner from third base by bunting. This strategy is called by a coach, since both you and the base runner must be in coordination. One attempt is called the *safety squeeze bunt.* You attempt to bunt down the first base line and the runner attempts to score. If you miss the ball, pop it up, or don't bunt, the runner can get back to his or her base. However, on a *suicide squeeze,* you must attempt to bunt the ball wherever it is pitched because the base runner is breaking with the pitch to come home. The strategy is to get the runner home before the ball can be fielded. Often both you and the runner will be safe.

Slow-Pitch Strategy

Hitting the ball into vacant spaces, called *place hitting,* is easier in slow-pitch play because the ball comes to the plate more slowly. Therefore, place hitting and power hitting are often more successful and should be practiced.

Batting Order

The order in which players are assigned to bat should be carefully determined. The first batter is often the shortest and fastest player on the team, a player who frequently gets on base. The second batter should be a good bunter or a hit-and-run hitter. A player should be able to advance the leadoff batter. The third, fourth, and fifth batters should be the most consistent and powerful hitters on the team. Their job is to bring home the earlier batters by hitting homers or extra-base hits. The weaker hitters follow. Usually the pitcher bats last.

The offensive team is permitted the option of using a designated hitter in fast-pitch play only. The DH becomes the tenth player in the lineup, although he or she may bat in any position so indicated at the start of the game and on the lineup sheet. The designated hitter may not enter the game on defense and should be an outstanding hitter.

The offensive team in slow pitch is permitted an extra hitter. The EH becomes the eleventh player in the lineup, although he or she may bat in any position as in fast pitch. An extra hitter may not enter the game on defense and should be an outstanding hitter. The extra hitter differs from a designated hitter in that the extra hitter is not a replacement hitter for a fielder who cannot bat.

Where is the "extra hitter" in slow-pitch softball placed in the lineup, and in what position may he or she bat?

Baserunning

At the crack of the bat, have one goal in mind—to get on base. Be alert and take advantage of any misplay to reach the farthest base. When you know you can reach first base safely, immediately round the base and look for the ball and the position of the fielders. If an error occurs, or if you realize that a defensive player cannot cover the base you are attempting to reach, continue running.

Once you are on base, your next goal is to advance around the bases to score a run. Your strategy now is to be aware of the game situation, the ability of the batter, the position of the fielders, and the number of outs. Be prepared to advance a base or more on any hit or error. Tag up on any long fly ball so that you may advance a base after the catch. Lead off partway on short fly balls or sinking fly balls in order to advance if the ball is not caught and/or to draw a throw. If you are on third base, stand with one foot on the base and the other in foul territory and move to foul territory as soon as it is legally possible to avoid being hit by a fair ball and being called out. With less than two outs:

1. Runner on first base and the ball is bunted to third base. Be alert to take third base if the catcher or pitcher does not cover the base while the third baseman fields the ball.
2. Runners on first and third base. On a short fly ball to the outfield, the runner on first should tag up and advance to draw the throw to second base so that the runner on third can score.
3. Runners on first and third. On a long fly ball to the outfield, the runner on third base should attempt to score; the runner on first should try to advance to second base if the long throw is made to home plate in an attempt to throw out the runner trying to score.
4. Runner on second base. If the ball is hit deep to the left side of the infield forcing a long throw to first base, try to advance to third base as soon as the ball leaves the fielder's hand.

When there are two outs, run to the next base as soon as the ball is hit. If you are caught in a rundown and are the lead runner with less than two out, attempt to make the next base and do not attempt to return to the original base. The trailing runner should be able to reach that base.

Coaching

As a base runner you should always watch the coach for signals that indicate you are to steal or run on a "hit-and-run" attempt, or if the batter is to bunt or "take a pitch." In addition, the coach will give you verbal and visual signals to guide decisions to go on, stop, tag up, or come back to a base.

Leading Off

Leading off is permitted in fast pitch and twelve-inch slow pitch only when the pitcher's nonpivot foot crosses the pitching plate. In sixteen-inch slow pitch, the batter may lead off at any time and can be "picked off" by the pitcher. The length of the leadoff should never exceed the ability to safely return after the ball is pitched in fast pitch and twelve-inch slow pitch and before the pitcher addresses the hitter in sixteen-inch play. In all fast-pitch situations, it is important that you look like you are going to steal on every pitch, and equally important when you stop your advance to immediately reverse your weight to the rear foot to avoid "leaning away" and thus losing balance for a fast return to base.

Substitute Players

Substitute or "pinch" hitters are used when a crucial scoring opportunity is at hand and a better hitter, bunter, or a more powerful hitter than the scheduled batter is available and needed. A pinch runner is used if the run is needed and the base runner is slow. The base runner is removed from the game, and a speedier runner is substituted. In fast-pitch and slow-pitch play, any of the starting players, except the DH in fast pitch or the EH in slow pitch, may be withdrawn and reenter once, provided such player occupies the same batting position, whenever he or she is in the lineup. However, a pitcher who is withdrawn cannot return to the pitching position for the remainder of the game. In addition, substitute fielders are used in the late innings by the leading team to remove a "good bat–weak glove person" for a stronger fielder.

In arranging a team's batting order, what are the abilities desired in each of the first five batters?

Defensive Patterns

Many defensive maneuvers are possible to counter offensive strategies. However, regardless of the defensive patterns used, if the offense executes its strategy correctly and accurately, it is very difficult, if not impossible, for the defensive patterns to work.

Fielding

The defensive team employs strategies to offset the offensive patterns of play. The following general rules should be followed:

1. Prevent the base runner from advancing a base. After a fly ball is caught, return the ball immediately to the base ahead of the runner. If a ground ball is hit, fake the runner back to the base before throwing out the batter–base runner. If you cannot throw ahead of the runner, throw the ball to a central position player such as the second baseman or pitcher.
2. Always make the sure out.
3. Always try for more than one out when there are runners on base.

Pitching is often considered the only defense a team has in softball. It is true that effective pitching will prevent base hits, but many base hits are gained simply because the fielders were not in proper position to protect their areas effectively. A good defensive team will alter its positions on the field to counter any offensive situation that might impair defensive efficiency.

There are times when the basic infield positions should be altered so that the infielders play closer or farther from home plate. These positions are called "back," "halfway," "close in," and "bunt." The *back position* is taken when there is no one on base. The infield and outfield play back, or deep, because the play probably will be to first base. This position enables the fielders to cover more territory. If the batter is left-handed, the infield and outfield shift about five steps toward the right-field line from their normal playing positions. The infielders play several steps behind the base paths.

The *halfway* or *pulled-in position* is assumed when there is a runner on first or second base with less than two outs. This position is also used when a bunt is expected or when the batter is a very fast runner. The halfway position allows for short, quick throws to prevent runners from advancing and also increases the possibility of a double play. In the halfway position, the outfielders move in a few steps, and the first and third basemen move several steps in front of the base path. The second baseman and the shortstop move in a step or two from regular position.

The *close-in position* is recommended when there is a runner on third base with less than two outs. This position enables the infield to field the ball rapidly so that they can hold runners on their bases or throw to home plate for an out. In the close in position the outfielders move in a few steps, the first and third basemen move approximately one-third the distance from the base path toward home plate, and the shortstop and second baseman move to the base path. If the runner on third is the winning run, the outfielders move closer to the infield. If the fielding team is several runs ahead, however, some teams prefer to play back and attempt to make the surest out even though a run may score.

The *bunt position* is assumed when a bunt is likely. It requires drastic repositioning by all players. The third baseman and first baseman must move in to almost one-third of the distance from home plate. Both the catcher and pitcher move toward the ball when it is bunted. The second baseman covers first base, the shortstop

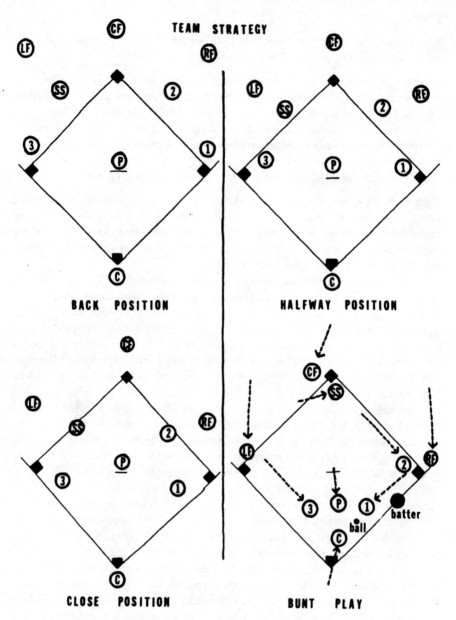

Figure 6.2
Defensive positions for fast pitch.

covers second base, and the left fielder covers third base for any possible plays at those bases.

Figure 6.2 illustrates these positions for fast-pitch play. In addition to shifting positions up and back and sideways, fielders must shift positions to cover bases not assigned to them and to back up plays. Techniques for backing and covering were discussed earlier. Since there are many possibilities, figures 6.3 to 6.13 illustrate where the fielders should move.

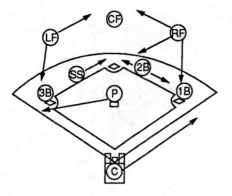

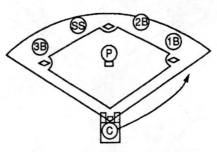

Figure 6.3
Covering and backing.

Figure 6.4
Catcher backing up a play. Play to first base. The catcher backs up the first baseman.

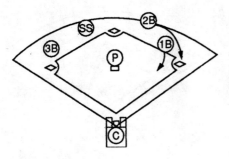

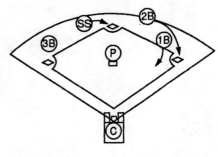

Figure 6.5
Covering first base. The second baseman covers first base when the first baseman must field the bunt.

Figure 6.6
Shortstop covering. When the second baseman must cover first base, the shortstop covers second base.

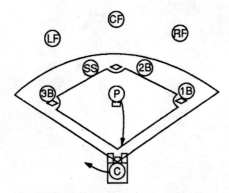

Figure 6.7
Pitcher covers home. The pitcher covers home when the catcher is drawn away.

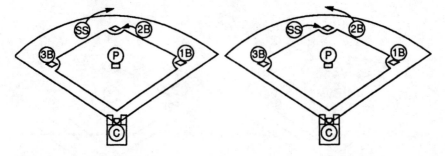

Figure 6.8
Action at second base. Shortstop backs up the second baseman when he/she covers the base, and the second baseman backs up the shortstop when he/she covers second base.

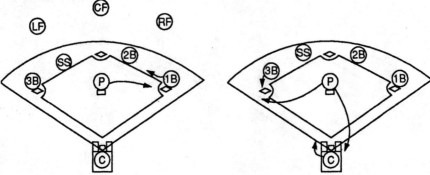

Figure 6.9
Pitcher covering first base. The pitcher covers first base when the first baseman must move to the right to field the ball.

Figure 6.10
Pitcher backing up a play. The pitcher backs up the third baseman on plays to third base and backs up the catcher on throws to home base.

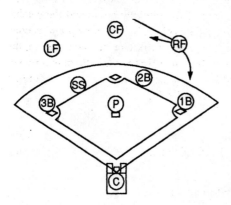

Figure 6.11
Right fielder backing up a play.

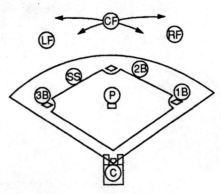

Figure 6.12
Center fielder backing up a play.

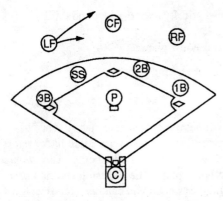

Figure 6.13
Left fielder backing up a play.

Covering and Backing Patterns

Many defensive errors are mental rather than physical errors, resulting from not backing up plays and covering bases properly. Practice is constantly needed to make these movements proper and routine. Teammates should shout directions and reminders to each other. Occasionally a timeout will be called to discuss the proper strategy on a possible play.

Under what circumstances should the infielders assume these positions: "back," "halfway," and "close-in"?

Bunt Coverage

Bunts are usually placed between home and the pitching circle, and along the foul lines. If the ball is rolling or spinning toward the foul line, it is better to let it roll foul. Touch it as soon as it reaches foul territory to make it a dead ball. Attempt to play all other bunts. When a bunt is anticipated, the first and third basemen assume a close-in position and charge the plate as soon as the batter appears to bunt. The pitcher should cover the area directly in front of the pitching circle and the catcher should cover the area immediately in front of the plate. The shortstop and second baseman will have three bases to cover. If there is no runner on second base, the shortstop covers second base and the second baseman first base. If there is a runner on second base, the shortstop covers third base and the second baseman covers first base. The bunt position is assumed when a bunt is likely.

Priority Plays

Fly balls travel across several positions. To eliminate any confusion, the following priorities are set:

1. Center fielders have priority over other fielders.
2. Outfielders have priority over infielders.
3. Other infielders have priority over pitchers and catchers.

4. The shortstop and second baseman have priority over the first and third basemen on hits behind their base.
5. Catchers have priority over balls hit near home plate.

Always signal visually and verbally that you are taking priority.

Cutoff Plays

Sometimes it can be judged that a throw will not put out the intended runner. Wherever this occurs it should be cut off and redirected to wherever a more likely out is possible or such an action would prevent a runner from advancing. Throws are most often cut off going to third base or to home plate. The shortstop and first baseman most often affect the cutoff and the third baseman and catcher usually call the play.

Practice

Individual

Mental Practice List possible playing situations and attempt to "think through" the play action that you should take from your playing position.

Group

Skill Sessions The coach or team leader should list various playing situations, both offensive and defensive, and request that players indicate what action they would take. Plays may be diagrammed and given to players to study.

Mock Setups Place the team on the field. The coach, manager, or team leader calls out or sets up various offensive situations for the defensive team to react to.

Bunt Reaction Drill Place infielders in their assigned positions. The coach preannounces the number of outs and the bases occupied. The pitcher pitches to the coach, who bunts. The players charge the bunt, field the ball, and other infielders cover and back up the proper bases. The ball is bunted in all directions. After three tries in each direction, the players switch positions.

Backing Up Practice All players take their positions. No ball is used. The coach identifies a situation and points where the ball is hit. All players react and move to their proper positions. Later, when the coach hits the ball, runners start from home and advance as in game conditions. Fielders will move to their proper fielding, covering, and backing positions.

Run-Down Practice Set up a situation between pairs of bases. Have the infielders make the play with proper positioning and backing up. The goal should be to complete the play with only two throws.

Rules and Unwritten Laws of the Game

7

Softball is governed essentially by one official set of rules, which include the following games: eleven- and twelve-inch slow pitch, fast pitch, sixteen-inch slow pitch, modified pitch, and coed play. In addition, after one hundred years, softball is also unofficially controlled by many unwritten rules.

Instructional Objectives

You will be able to—

1. play softball according to the official rules, and
2. understand and follow unwritten softball rules.

Rules of the Game

Prior to 1980, all softball rules were under the jurisdiction of the International Joint Rule Committee on Softball. Since that time they have been under the jurisdiction of the Amateur Softball Association. A committee for each type of game sets the rules. Each committee has representation from the various game committees, the ASA umpires, and allied organizations. These committees meet annually to review softball playing rules and to make any needed changes. The rules identified in this chapter represent what was current at the time of writing. Permission to copy the rules must be given by the ASA. A complete set of rules can be secured from local sporting goods dealers, bookstores, or from your local library.

Since the official rules are written as one set of rules, exceptions or special rules governing fast- and slow-pitch play are noted within a rule. It is essential that the official ASA rules be reviewed for a particular type of play.

The Playing Field

Softball should be played in a clear and unobstructed area within a radius that varies by gender, age, and type of play. The distance ranges from 300 feet for slow-pitch super play, to 175 feet for girls ten years old and under, from home plate between foul lines. Pitching distances vary from 50 feet for slow-pitch adult play to 35 feet for fast pitch, age ten and under. Figures 7.1 and 7.2 present the official distances for the playing field for all types of play. When deviations from these dimensions must be made, special ground rules may be agreed upon.

OFFICIAL DIMENSIONS
FOR SOFTBALL DIAMONDS
Prepared by The Amateur Softball Association

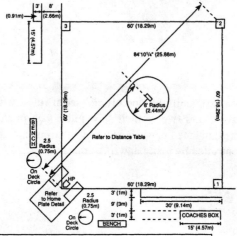

DISTANCE TABLE

ADULT

GAME	DIVISION	BASES	PITCHING	FENCES
Fast Pitch	Women	60' (18.29m)	40' (12.19m)	200' (60.96m)
	Men	60' (18.29m)	46' (14.02m)	250' (76.20m)
	Jr. Men	60' (18.29m)	46' (14.02m)	250' (76.20m)
Modified	Women	60' (18.29m)	40' (12.19m)	200' (60.96m)
	Men	60' (18.29m)	46' (14.02m)	265' (80.80m)
Slow Pitch	Women	65' (19.81m)	50' (15.24m)	250' (76.20m)
	Men	65' (19.81m)	50' (15.24m)	275' (83.82m)
	Co-Ed	65' (19.81m)	50' (15.24m)	275' (83.82m)
	Super	65' (19.81m)	50' (15.24m)	300' (91.44m)
16 Inch	Women	55' (16.76m)	38' (11.58m)	200' (60.96m)
Slow Pitch	Women	55' (16.76m)	38' (11.58m)	250' (76.20m)

YOUTH

GAME	DIVISION	BASES	PITCHING	FENCES Minimum	Maximum
Slow Pitch	Girls 10-under	55' (16.76m)	35' (10.67m)	150' (45.72m)	175' (53.34m)
	Boys 10-under	55' (16.76m)	35' (10.67m)	150' (45.72m)	175' (53.34m)
	Girls 12-under	60' (18.29m)	40' (12.19m)	175' (53.34m)	200' (60.96m)
	Boys 12-under	60' (18.29m)	40' (12.19m)	175' (53.34m)	200' (60.96m)
	Girls 14-under	65' (19.81m)	46' (14.02m)	225' (68.58m)	250' (76.20m)
	Boys 14-under	65' (19.81m)	46' (14.02m)	250' (76.20m)	275' (83.82m)
	Girls 16-under	65' (19.81m)	46' (14.02m)	225' (68.58m)	250' (76.20m)
	Boys 16-under	65' (19.81m)	46' (14.02m)	275' (83.82m)	300' (91.44m)
	Girls 18-under	65' (19.81m)	50' (15.24m)	225' (68.58m)	250' (76.20m)
	Boys 18-under	65' (19.81m)	50' (15.24m)	275' (83.82m)	300' (91.44m)
Fast Pitch	Girls 10-under	55' (16.76m)	35' (10.67m)	150' (45.72m)	175' (53.34m)
	Boys 10-under	55' (16.76m)	35' (10.67m)	150' (45.72m)	175' (53.34m)
	Girls 12-under	60' (18.29m)	35' (10.67m)	175' (53.34m)	200' (60.96m)
	Boys 12-under	60' (18.29m)	40' (12.19m)	175' (53.34m)	200' (60.96m)
	Girls 14-under	60' (18.29m)	40' (12.19m)	175' (53.34m)	200' (60.96m)
	Boys 14-under	60' (18.29m)	46' (14.02m)	175' (53.34m)	200' (60.96m)
	Girls 16-under	60' (18.29m)	40' (12.19m)	200' (60.96m)	225' (68.58m)
	Boys 16-under	60' (18.29m)	46' (14.02m)	200' (60.96m)	225' (68.58m)
	Girls 18-under	60' (18.29m)	40' (12.19m)	200' (60.96m)	225' (68.58m)
	Boys 18-under	60' (18.29m)	46' (14.02m)	200' (60.96m)	225' (68.58m)

Figure 7.1
Official dimensions for softball diamonds.

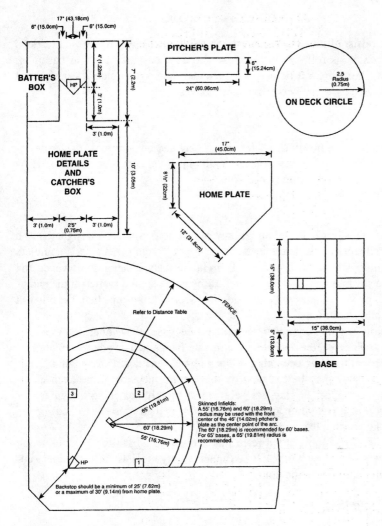

Figure 7.2
Dimensions.

Players and Substitutes

Most of the players of various positions for fast- and slow-pitch play are similar. Each player traditionally covers a certain specified area but may be stationed anywhere on fair ground, except for the pitcher, who must be in legal pitching position, and the catcher, who must be in his or her box. Substitute players may be used, but once removed from the game a player may not return. Substitute players may be put in the game for a batter, fielder, runner, or pitcher. The position of a player may be altered at any time during a game, but a substitute player must assume the position in the batting order of the player he or she replaced.

Fast Pitch

A team shall consist of nine (fast pitch) or ten (slow pitch) players whose positions shall be designated as follows: pitcher, catcher, first baseman, second baseman, third baseman, shortstop, left fielder, center fielder, and right fielder. A designated hitter (DH) may be used and becomes a tenth player.

Slow Pitch

A team consists of nine positions in slow-pitch play and an additional player designated as a short fielder. In addition, an eleventh player called an extra hitter (EH) is allowed to bat but not play defensively.

The Game

The home team bats last in each inning; however, if neither team is designated as a "home" team, the choice is determined by the toss of a coin. A game is complete when seven innings have been played. If the home team is leading, however, the last half of the seventh inning is not played. If the game should be tied at the end of seven innings, play continues until one side has scored more runs than the other at the end of a complete inning.

Occasionally a game cannot be completed because of weather, darkness, or calamities. In such cases, the decision to terminate the game is made by the umpire. If five or more innings have been played, the game is considered a regulation, completed game. A game may be forfeited by the umpire in favor of the team not at fault for failure to appear to play, for delaying or unduly hastening the game, for willful violation of a rule after warning, or for fewer than nine (fast pitch) or ten (slow pitch) players on a team.

The winner of the game is the team that scores the most runs in a regulation game. One run is scored each time a base runner legally touches each base consecutively before the third out of the inning.

Pitching Regulations

The game starts when the umpire calls "Play!" The first batter steps into the batter's box, the catcher readies himself or herself in the catcher's box. The ball may be held no less than one second or more than ten seconds. The pitcher may use any windup provided he or she does not make any motion to pitch without immediately delivering the ball to the batter, use a rocker action, make more than one revolution of the arm, make any motion that results in a reversal of the forward action or continue to wind up after taking the forward step.

Fast Pitch

The pitcher in fast pitch takes a position with pivot foot on the pitcher's plate and nonpivot foot on or behind the pitcher's plate.

Slow Pitch

One or both feet must be in contact with the pitcher's plate. The ball must be delivered at a moderate speed with a perceptible arc (from the time it leaves the pitcher's hand) of at least six feet before the ball reaches home plate.

Batting Regulations

When the pitch is delivered, the batter must decide whether or not to swing the bat at the ball in an attempt to hit it. If the pitch is not struck at, the umpire decides whether the pitch is a ball or a strike. If the batter incurs three strikes, he or she is called out; conversely, if the batter acquires four balls, he or she is entitled to first base and becomes a base runner. If the pitcher delivers the ball illegally by dropping, rolling, or bouncing the ball to prevent the batter from striking it, or if tape or other substances are used on the ball, a ball is called on the batter. In the fast-pitch game only, base runners are permitted to advance one base.

If the batter elects to swing at the pitch and misses it, a strike is called. A foul ball is declared if the ball is hit but lands outside the lines defining the playing field. When a foul ball is not caught on the fly, a strike is called unless the batter already has two strikes. In this case any number of foul balls may be hit without a strike being called in fast pitch. In slow-pitch play, a foul ball not caught is always a strike including the third strike. A foul tip is called if the ball is hit and goes directly back to the catcher's hands and is held by the catcher. A foul tip is a strike regardless of the number of strikes on the batter. When a fly ball is caught, whether it is in fair or foul territory, the batter is out. If the batter hits the ball on the ground into fair territory, he or she must reach first base before the ball can be held by the first baseman while touching the bag, or be declared out.

Each team is given three outs during its time at bat. The batter is out when any of the following situations occur: when three strikes are called and the ball is held by the catcher; when a foul ball is legally caught; immediately when he or she hits an infield fly with base runners on first and second or first, second, and third bases with less than two outs. This rule prevents a defensive team from setting up a forced double play. However, the batter is out if the ball is bunted into foul territory after two strikes in fast pitch. In slow pitch, the batter is out if he or she attempts to bunt or chop down on the ball.

Baserunning Regulations

The batter becomes a base runner as soon as a ball is hit into fair territory, or when four balls have been called, or when the catcher interferes with or prevents the batter from striking a pitched ball. In addition, in fast pitch the batter becomes a base runner when hit by a pitched ball or when the catcher drops the third strike when no one is on base or in any situation when there are two outs. Bases must be touched consecutively. Two base runners may not occupy the same base. The right to a base is given to the runner who first occupied it, and he or she is entitled to hold that base until he or she has legally touched the next base or until forced to vacate it for a succeeding runner.

The base runner is entitled to advance with liability to be put out when the heel of the pitcher's nonpivot foot crosses the front edge of the pitcher's plate on the forward step on a pitch (fast pitch only), when the ball is overthrown into fair or foul territory and is not blocked, when the ball is batted into fair territory and is not blocked, and when a legally caught fly ball is first touched. In the fast-pitch game, leading off is legal after the ball leaves the pitcher's hand. However, the base runner must return to the base if he or she does not steal once the pitcher has the ball within the eight-foot radius of the pitcher's plate.

Base runners are entitled to advance to another base and may not be put out in the following situations: when forced to vacate a base because the batter was awarded a base on balls, when a fielder obstructs the base runner's path, when the catcher interferes with the batter, and when a pitcher or overthrown ball in foul territory is blocked or obstructed. In addition, base runners may advance without being put out if the batter is awarded a base because he or she was hit by a pitched ball, when a wild pitch or passed ball goes under, over, or through the backstop, and when the pitcher pitches illegally.

Under what circumstances in fast-pitch softball does the batter become a baserunner without having hit a fair ball?

There are times when a base runner is restricted to a certain number of bases. For example, if the fence is less than the prescribed distance from home base, a ball falling beyond it will entitle the runner to only two bases. If the fence is regulation distance, but the ball rolls or bounds into a stand or over, under, or through a fence or other obstruction marking the boundaries, two bases are awarded. When the team at bat commits an illegal act, a base runner cannot advance on the play. Thus, if a ball is illegally batted or if the batter interferes with a play, no advance is permitted. To protect the defensive team, if the umpire is struck by a batted ball before it is touched by a fielder or if the plate umpire interferes with the catcher's attempt to throw, no advance is permitted.

A base runner is declared out if he or she is not standing on a base and is touched by a fielder who is holding the ball or is forced to advance and fails to reach that base before the ball is held on that base by a fielder. A base runner also will be called out if he or she runs the base in reverse order, fails to return to his or her base when play is resumed after a suspension of play, passes a preceding base runner, leaves a base before a fly ball has been caught, fails to touch a base, is struck by a batted ball, or interferes with the fielding of a batted ball.

Official Rules

The ASA Official Rules are most often used to govern play. These rules specify variations for the following levels of play: adult fast pitch and slow pitch for men and women; slow pitch for coed; super play, modified, and sixteen-inch slow pitch for men and women; and for youth, play for slow and fast pitch for boys and girls ages twelve and under, fifteen and under, and eighteen and under. Because of these variations, it is important that you obtain the latest official rule book to be able to play *your* game according to the correct rules.

However, two variations are so different that they are worth pointing out.

Coed Play

The ASA Rules Committee has developed rules governing coed slow-pitch softball play. Essentially these rules call for foul lines three hundred feet from home plate to the fence, fifty feet pitching distance, no metal or hard plastic spikes, and ten players. The ten players must include five males and five females playing at all times. In addition, there must be two of each gender in the outfield and in the infield. The battery shall consist of one male and one female. The batting order must alternate each batter by gender.

Sixteen-Inch Slow Pitch

The sixteen-inch slow-pitch game permits base runners to lead off base and pitchers to use hesitations before delivering the ball to the batter. During these hesitations, the pitcher may attempt to pick off a runner as in baseball. In addition, the bases are fifty-five feet apart, and the pitching distance is only thirty-eight feet from home plate.

Officiating

The rules of the game are enforced by one or more umpires. They have the power to order a player or coach to act in any manner that, in their judgment, is necessary to give force and effect to one or all of the rules. An umpire must not be connected in any way with either team. If there are two umpires, each has the power to make decisions on violations committed anytime during time or during suspension of play. One umpire rules from behind the plate and the other from the bases. The plate umpire has full charge and is responsible for the conduct of the game. The plate umpire makes decisions on the pitches and the action of the batter. The base umpire renders decisions at all bases except at home plate. In tournament play, usually an umpire is assigned to each base.

Both the ASA and the NAGWS sponsor programs to prepare, assist, and regulate umpiring in softball. Questions concerning rules should be sent to The Amateur Softball Association, 2801 NE 50th Street, Oklahoma City, Oklahoma, 73111.

Scorekeeping

The rules specifically outline procedures and regulations for scorekeeping. The official scorer records and summarizes the game activities as they relate to final score, runs batted in, hits, extra–base hits, stolen bases, sacrifice bunts and flies, double plays, triple plays, runners left on base, bases on balls, strikeouts, wild pitches, passed balls, name of the winning pitcher, name of losing pitcher, names of umpires, and length of the game.

Sample Game

White City is playing Greenville at Greenville. Since Greenville is playing in its hometown, it is considered the home team and will bat last in each inning. The umpires arrive thirty minutes before the game to become familiar with the playing field and the teams.

Just before play begins, the umpires meet with the managers and team captains to go over ground rules. At the time designated to begin the game, the home team assumes its playing field positions. The visiting team bats first and in the order listed on the official batting lineup. The first batter hits the ball on the ground to the third baseman. He or she throws the ball to the first baseman who, while holding the ball, touches the bag ahead of the batter–base runner. This of course is an out. The next batter hits the ball over the shortstop's head; the ball lands before the left fielder can catch it. The left fielder knows the ball cannot get to first base before the batter–base runner, so he throws the ball to the second baseman to prevent the runner from taking an additional base. The next batter receives four balls and is given first base. The runner on first is allowed to take second base. On the next pitch, the batter hits a fly ball, which is caught by the second baseman. There are now two outs. After taking two strikes, the sixth batter hits a ball that the center fielder drops for an error. The base runner on second scores on the error, and the batter–base runner gets to second base while the runner on first base stops at third. The last batter hits a foul ball that is caught by the catcher. This completes the first half of the first inning. The game continues in this manner until completed.

Unwritten Laws

Many softball procedures are accepted by players and fans alike, even though they are not listed in the official rules. Protesting close decisions made by the umpire, shouting words of encouragement, and taunting the opposition are acceptable. Players often follow certain superstitions and employ procedures and tactics that might delay or speed up the game.

Conduct of the Game

Protesting decisions is usually considered poor sportsmanship in most athletic endeavors, but in softball such protests are accepted as part of the color of the game in nonschool game situations. Usually these protests do not result in a changed decision. Complaints are actually expected by fans, players, and officials. In educational settings, coaches and teachers should discourage adherence to the preceding unwritten law. Protesting too vigorously or using physical violence will result, however, in the offender's being ejected from the game by the umpire. This behavior is not considered sportsmanlike.

Shouting words of encouragement by teammates to the pitcher or the batter is expected and desirable. Occasionally, disparaging remarks are made about the opposing pitcher or batter. These are not considered proper.

Stopping play to discuss the course of action to be taken is legal and is expected in certain situations. The manager may stop play to discuss offensive strategy with his or her batter, or may choose to stop play to discuss defensive strategy when his or her team is in the field. Opposing fans usually boo mildly at these delays but cheer such delays when they are employed by their coaches. The rules limit conferences with the manager or other representatives from the dugout to one per inning.

Conferences occasionally are designed merely to delay the game for a psychological effect. A meeting of the pitcher and catcher is often held to give the pitcher a chance to calm down and rest or to "cool off" the opposition if they have been hitting the pitcher too frequently. The batter tries to annoy the pitcher by meeting with his or her coach or by stepping out of the batting box frequently.

Many players follow certain superstitions that they are certain affect the outcome of the game. For example, some players when running out to their defensive positions feel that they will have bad luck if they don't step on a certain base or hitch their belts before every new batter comes to bat.

Miscellaneous Laws

Rubbing dirt on the bat is done to dry perspiration so that the bat will not slip from the hands. The pitcher often uses rosin on his or her hands for the same reason.

The next batter to bat is said to be "on deck." When on deck, the player kneels halfway between the bench and plate, warmed up and ready to take his or her turn.

If the pitcher gets on base, play usually is stopped to give the pitcher his or her jacket. This is done to keep his or her pitching arm warm so it will not tighten up.

Throwing a bat is dangerous. Players should drop the bat and run to first base when the ball is hit. The bat should not be thrown unnecessarily or in anger.

Most teams wear uniforms to identify themselves with their team. These uniforms are usually the traditional baseball uniform or slacks.

Playing the Game

8

Softball provides action and excitement that may lead to awards and national and international recognition. Competition is provided on a local, regional, state, national, and international basis.

Instructional Objectives

You will be able to—

1. get into condition and improve your game performance,
2. find opportunities to play softball,
3. secure information about current softball developments.

Self-Evaluation

If you wish to develop skill as a softball player, you should know what skill looks like. Try to watch experts play. Read books or articles written about the position you play as well as about the game in general. Set batting, baserunning, and fielding goals for yourself. Know your batting average. You can figure it by dividing the total number of hits you have made by the total number of times you have been at bat. A batting average of .300 or more is considered excellent. Fielding average is computed by dividing your total putouts and assists by your total putouts, assists, and errors. A fielding average of .970 or better is considered excellent. Clock your running time from home to first and from home to the other bases. Constantly strive to improve that time.

No matter how much you know about softball or how much you practice, your progress toward increased ability in performing softball skills depends on how much effort and time you are willing to give.

How rapidly you master the skills of softball depends on many factors. Needless to say, every athlete would like to find a shortcut to the acquisition of skill. Most, however, would agree that there is no quick, simple way to stardom, but there are some steps that can speed up progress. The first step is to be in top physical condition so that you have the agility, endurance and strength necessary to perform softball techniques. Conditioning is the foundation for perfecting skills. The real work is practice. Individual and group practice, faithfully pursued, will increase skill. In addition, a softball player must study the game and study himself or herself. Only by knowing all the finer points of the game and understanding your own strengths and weaknesses can you intelligently progress toward real skill in playing softball.

Conditioning

Conditioning has three major aspects: physical, nutritional, and psychological. These are interdependent, each depending on the other for optimal performance.

Physical

To be an expert softball player you must possess arm and shoulder strength for throwing and hitting. Endurance and speed are important to fielding and baserunning. Timing, agility, and accuracy are necessary for batting and throwing. Exercise and practice should be pursued beyond the initial point of fatigue if improvement is to be expected. Exercises used for most sports have application to conditioning for softball. As in any sport, however, the exercises should relate to the specific sport. The exercises should not only relate to increasing strength but also to improving joint flexibility to avoid injuries. In addition, the use of proper mechanics of the body when performing the various skills will also protect against injury. Table 8.1 provides information concerning protection and strengthening of specific body areas used in performing softball skills. Consult a fitness book for further details for the development of strength and flexibility. Develop your own series of conditioning exercises and do them daily. Do not be content with merely doing the same amount each day. Set goals for yourself to improve your strength, speed, and the distance and accuracy of your throws.

In addition to these general conditioning exercises it is recommended that you practice with a weighted bat, weighted ball, and wrist snap bat.

Weighted Bats

These can be made by drilling a hole in the barrel and adding lead, or by attaching a weight batting ring. Practice swinging with a weighted bat; this helps to increase the strength of the muscles involved in the swing. The ASA rules limit warming up before officially batting to the use of two official softball bats at once or one ASA approved *warm-up bat*. Official warm-up bats are so marked, weigh a minimum of forty-eight ounces and have a 2½-inch diameter barrel, a no more than 15-inch safety grip, and are of one-piece construction. These bats are also good for pregame swing practice.

Weighted Balls

Throwing a heavier ball several times daily will increase your arm strength. A ball can be made heavier by soaking it in water or wrapping tape around it. Increase the distance from the target when speed and accuracy are attained from a particular distance.

Table 8.1 CONDITIONING

Area	Exercises		
	Strength	*Flexibility*	*Mechanics*
Arm and shoulders	Push-ups	Stretching and bending arms to and from the chest	Stride in direction of the throw. Open hips toward the target. Arm lags behind trunk rotation. Follow through.
Legs and hips	Running 15/20 minutes Rope jumping 15/20 minutes	Hamstring stretching Bent-leg stretches Alternate strides	Center body over feet. Don't overstride. Shift weight rear to front.
Hand strength	Squeeze small rubber ball.	Force fingers backward several times.	Give when ball hits glove. Fingers point down for below-waist catch. Fingers point up for above-waist catch.

Wrist Snap Bats

Wrist snap is important for developing power when batting. A wrist snap bat has a ball attached by a nylon cord placed through a hole in the center of the ball and one and a half inches from the end of the bat, about six inches from the barrel end. As you swing the bat, the ball will flip in front of the bat as you snap your wrists. This action provides you with feedback regarding the effectiveness of your wrist action.

Imagine yourself in your usual position on the fielding team. There is one out and a runner on first. Can you self-talk to effectively prepare for what may happen with the next batter?

Nutritional

Exercising without control of the diet will ultimately be counterproductive. Proper nutrition means controlling the quantity and quality of what you eat. The quantity of what you eat can be controlled by at least weighing yourself weekly.

Like computing your batting average, it will tell you whether your food intake is too much or too little. The adjustment in quantity should be equally distributed in the kinds of foods that you eat . . . the quality. Quality nutrition means eating some fruit, vegetables, meat or fish, breads or cereals, and milk.

Psychological

Concentration and anxiety control are essential to optimal performance. Concentration can be aided by using *self-talk* and *imagery*. Self-talk is talking to yourself about where you should play, what to expect, what you plan to do, and how you wish to feel. Imagery is rehearsing in your mind the exact sequences of a skill, the feeling of a perfectly executed swing or catch and/or the visual "seeing" yourself performing perfectly. Anxiety may aid or harm performance. Accuracy-type skills need less stress; power skills, like running bases, need more stress. Too much stress can be controlled by using the relaxation techniques of deep breathing or alternately tensing and releasing the muscles of the body. The psyching up that can result from cheering, clapping, and bounding up and down adds more stress and power.

Design a personal conditioning program to prepare yourself for a season of softball playing.

Competitive Play

Softball competition begins with the friendly game at the park and ends with World Softball Tournaments for all levels of play. Between these extremes are intramural softball, interscholastic and intercollegiate play, church leagues, park leagues, and industrial play. Many nonschool teams are commercially sponsored.

Umpiring and Scorekeeping

9

Quality softball play requires quality umpiring and scorekeeping. After learning about softball, you may wish to become an umpire or scorekeeper.

Instructional Objectives

You will be able to—

1. umpire softball games, and
2. keep score for softball games.

Umpiring

Umpiring is a difficult task but it can be enjoyable and rewarding. A thorough understanding of the rules governing play and umpiring, ability to maintain alertness, exercising patience, and making consistent and accurate judgments are essential. Sponsoring agencies such as leagues, associations, or tournaments usually set the minimum standards that govern the quality of umpiring. Obviously less rigor is demanded in "sandlot" play or in physical education classes than in interschool, league, or tournament competition. Umpires are assigned to a particular game by the organizations they represent.

Number and Position of Umpires

The major function of umpiring is to enforce the rules as they relate to batting, pitching, fielding, and baserunning. The number of umpires used in a game depends on the quality of play. Most games use two umpires. However, a minimum of three umpires are recommended in tournament play.

Major duties are to judge the pitches and hits and render base decisions. When more than one umpire is used, one is called the plate umpire and the other, the base umpire. They both are empowered to order the commission and omission of any act that in their judgment is necessary to comply with the rules.

General Information

The rules clearly identify the duties and responsibilities of umpires. Umpires are expected to wear uniforms consisting of powder-blue shirts and dark navy-blue pants. The plate umpire must wear a mask with a throat protector and body protector in fast-pitch softball and their use is recommended in slow-pitch play. In addition, the plate umpire needs a ball and strike indicator, a whisk broom, and a ball bag. Each umpire should have a copy of the official rules available.

Umpires should confer with each other, coaches, managers, and scorekeepers before the game begins. The plate umpire collects the games balls and returns them to the owner, and often checks the scorebook with the scorekeeper. All questions should be answered politely during and after the game. The following suggestions will contribute to quality umpiring:

1. Display dignified manner.
2. Call plays consistently, fairly, promptly, and accurately.
3. Try to anticipate play to be ready for action.
4. Correct errors promptly.
5. Avoid arguments and making personal comments.
6. Be aloof and apart from players, coaches, managers, and spectators.
7. Use signals and call out decisions loudly.
8. Attend clinics to update and improve your ability to umpire.

Each umpire has the power to make decisions on violations committed at any time until the game is over. Neither umpire can set aside or question decisions made by the other within the limits of their respective duties. Umpires may consult each other, but the final decision rests with the umpire whose exclusive authority it was to make the decision. All umpires have equal authority to call a runner out for leaving a base too soon; call TIME; remove players, coaches, or managers; and call illegal pitches.

Pregame Duties

Umpires should arrive twenty to thirty minutes before the game is to begin. Prior to the game, you as an umpire should ready your equipment, check the playing area to determine needed ground rules, and check with the official scorekeeper and the other umpire. A pregame conference is conducted at home plate with the team captains and managers to receive the lineup cards, go over the ground rules, clarify any needed rule interpretation, and indicate expected player behavior.

Plate Umpire

The plate umpire is considered to be the umpire in chief and is in full charge of the proper conduct of the game. He or she is positioned one or two feet behind the catcher in a crouched position that will not interfere with the catcher's ability to view the plate, batter, pitcher, foul lines, bases and field (see figure 9.1). Duties of the plate umpire are as follows:

1. Call balls and strikes.
2. Call hit balls, fair or foul.
3. Call legal or illegal pitches and catches.
4. Call base play if the base umpire leaves the infield.

Figure 9.1
Plate umpire position.

5. Judge whether a ball is bunted, chopped, or touches the batter or clothing of the batter.
6. Judge a fly ball as in the infield or outfield.
7. Determine when a game is forfeited.
8. Assume all duties when assigned as a single umpire.
9. Rule on fitness of field for play in case of rain or other problems.
10. Rectify any situation in which the reversal of an umpire's decision or a delayed call by an umpire places a batter-runner or a base runner in jeopardy.

Position

The plate umpire moves into a slight crouch when the pitcher steps on the rubber and assumes a readiness-to-pitch position. Eyes should be fixed on the pitcher and the ball. The body should be aligned with the pitch. Crouch lower, straighter, or higher to align the body with the pitch. On a batted ball, the plate umpire takes a position in foul territory, no more than five feet down the baseline, in the direction of the next possible play. Umpires may rotate as provided in the rules.

Controlling the Game

The following procedures will contribute to a smooth and safe conduct of the game:

1. Encourage players to hustle on and off the field.
2. Discourage lengthy conferences between players and/or coaches.
3. Limit warm-up pitches to five.
4. Brush the plate between innings and at any other time when needed.
5. Keep the field clear of debris, bats, loose material and spectators.
6. Keep "on deck" batter ready in designated waiting area.
7. Suspend or discontinue play when the field or weather conditions present a hazard.

Figure 9.2
Base umpire position.

What are the umpires' responsibilities before and during the game in regard to the condition of the field?

Base Umpire

The base umpire renders all decisions at bases except those made by the plate umpire. In addition, the base umpire assists the plate umpire in enforcing the rules. (See figure 9.2.)

Position

Because of the differences in leadoff and base-stealing rules between slow- and fast-pitch softball, the positions of base umpires vary somewhat. Details of these differences can be found in official umpiring manuals. Proper position of the base umpire changes with varying playing situations. When no one is on base, the umpire should stand ten to fifteen feet beyond the first base with the right foot beside the foul line in foul territory. If the ball is hit to the left side of the infield, the base umpire moves to fair territory ten to fifteen feet from first base and slightly outside of the first to second base path facing first base. If the batter-runner advances toward second base, the base umpire moves toward the inside of the infield and stays with the runner. Generally, if the ball goes outside the infield, the base umpire must go inside of the base path, and if the ball stays inside of the infield, the umpire stays outside of the base path. If the ball is hit to the outfield, the umpire moves to a spot about five feet to the infield side of the base line between first and second base.

With a runner on first base, the umpire moves to a position between first and second base, outside of the base path. The base umpire needs to maintain a position that allows good perspective of both the pitcher and base runners. It is imperative that the position assumed does not obstruct the vision of an outfielder or impede the movements of an infielder. On a tag play, the umpire should be within five feet of the play and focus attention on the baseman, not the base.

Situation	Umpire Signals	
	Verbal Signal	*Visual Signal*
Begin or resume play	Play ball	Motion to pitcher.
Strike	Strike	Raise right hand upward.
Ball	Ball	No arm signal
Give count	Call balls first	None
Foul balls	Foul ball	Extend arm horizontally away from diamond.
Fair ball	None	Extend arm in a pumping motion toward the diamond.
Out	None	Raise right arm and hand over right shoulder with fingers closed.
Safe	None	Extend both arms diagonally in front of body with palms facing the ground.
Suspension of play	Time	Extend both arms above head.
Delayed dead ball	None	Extend left arm horizontally.
Trapped ball	None	Same as safe
Ground rule double	None	Extend right hand above head with two fingers extended.
Home run	None	Extend right hand with closed fingers above head and circle arm in clockwise direction.

Practice

Most organizations that sponsor or control league or tournament play provide clinics and workshops designed to develop and improve umpiring. The Amateur Softball Association and the National Association for Girls' and Women's Sports promote clinics, provide detailed information about umpiring, and offer programs for official ratings. Attending these events and assisting in less competitive games are excellent ways to improve ability in umpiring.

Signals

Most single decisions are indicated with both a visual and verbal signal.

What is the base umpire's proper position under each of these circumstances: no one is on base; the ball is hit to the outfield; the batter-runner advances toward second base?

Scorekeeping

The scorekeeper (figure 9.3) should have a thorough knowledge of the rules and techniques of the games and the ability to make decisions and attend to details.

The duties of the scorekeeper are to keep all records of each game as outlined in the official rules. It is the scorer's responsibility to officially determine playing

Figure 9.3
Scorekeeper.

errors, base hits, runs batted in, pitching credit for winning or losing, stolen bases, passed balls, and wild pitches. The scorer shall not make decisions that conflict with official playing rules or with the umpire's decisions.

Scoresheet

The scoresheet (see figure 9.4) must be completed so that it is possible to reconstruct the official action of the game from which a box score and summary of the game can be prepared. There are many ways to record official action in a game. Some scorekeepers construct their own systems. Any system may be used providing game action is accurately recorded and can be retrieved by other readers.

Each player's name and the position or positions played shall be listed in the order in which he or she batted or would have batted. In fast pitch, the DH is optional, but if one is to be used, it must be made known prior to the start of the game and listed on the scoresheet in the regular batting order. Ten names will be listed, with the tenth name being the player playing defense only. The same is true for the EH in slow pitch; however, all players will bat but the eleventh player will not play on defense.

Box Score

The box score should include each player's name and position and order of batting. The following information shall be recorded for each play: batting and fielding records including times at bat, runs, base hits, putouts, assists, entry, and errors.

Summary

The summary of the game shall list the following information:

1. The score by innings and the final score.
2. The run batted in and by whom hit. (RBI)
3. Two-base hits and by whom hit. (2B)

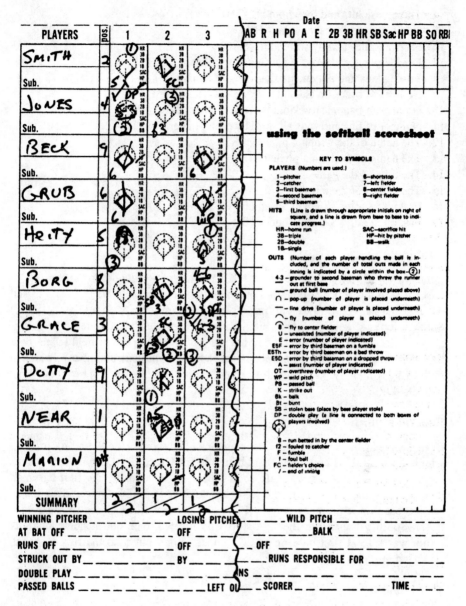

Figure 9.4
Scoresheet.

4. Three-base hits and by whom hit. (3B)
5. Home runs and by whom hit. (HR)
6. Sacrifice flies and by whom hit. (SAC)
7. Double plays and players participating in them. (DP)
8. Triple plays and players participating in them. (TP)
9. Number of bases on balls given by each pitcher. (BB)
10. Number of batters struck out by each pitcher. (K)
11. Number of hits and runs allowed by each pitcher. (H) (R)
12. The name of the winning pitcher. (WP)
13. The name of the losing pitcher. (LP)
14. The time of the game.
15. The names of the umpires and scorers.
16. Fast pitch only: Stolen bases and by whom. (SB)
17. Fast pitch only: Sacrifice bunts. (Bt)

First Inning

Smith was walked (BB). (Line through BB.) Jones hit a grounder to the third baseman (5) who threw out Smith at second base on a double play (DP) (4) who tossed
out Jones at first base (3). (Join Smith's and Jones's boxes with a line ├─────┤.)
Smith ① Jones ② were out. (Outs are marked by a number with a circle.) Beck sin-
gled to right field (1B). Grub hit a home run (HR) over the center field fence (note
line indicating area). Two runs were batted in by third baseman number 6, which is
marked by (6). Heity hit a fly ball to center field ⑧ for the third out ③. Two runs,
two hits. 2/2.

Second Inning

Borg doubles (2B) to left field. Grace singles (1B) to right field, batting in Borg
who had stolen third base (SB). Run batted in for Grace (3). Dotty struck out for
the first out (K) ①. Near was safe at first base on an error by the first baseman
who dropped the throw from the third baseman (AF, E3D). Grace advanced to
second base on a fielder's choice (FC). Marion sacrificed Grace to third base
(Sac). Smith grounded to the shortstop who threw Grace out at home plate ②.
Smith was safe at first base on a (FC). Jones fouled out ③ to the first baseman
(f3). One run, two hits. 1/2.

Third Inning

Beck singles to left field (1B). Grub tripled to right field (3B) scoring Beck. Run
batted in for Grub (6). Grub scored on a wild pitch (WP). Heity popped out to the
third baseman ⑤ for the first out ①. Borg was hit by a pitched ball (HP). Grace hit a
grounder to the second baseman who throws out Borg at second base ②, 4–6, on a
throw to the shortstop who throws out Borg at first base to complete a double play
③, 6–3. Two runs, two hits. 2/2.

Summary of the Box Score

Figure 9.4 does not show a complete game. However, the summary will list the following:

1. runs and hits in each inning by each team,
2. the name of the winning and losing pitcher,
3. number of batters faced,
4. times each batter was at bat,
5. hits and runs scored by each batter,
6. pitcher's number of strikeouts, base on balls, innings pitched, wild pitches, balks and batters hit by pitched ball, and earned runs,
7. number of double plays by each team and by which players, and
8. number of passed balls and by whom and the time of the game.

Qualifications of Umpires

An ASA umpire must pass a written examination that qualifies him or her to register with both the state and national ASA. Annual dues must be paid to each association. In return, the umpire receives a copy of the current ASA Official Rule Book, a copy of the Case Book, an arm patch, an umpire card, and accident insurance.

Coaching and Managing

10

Your progress may be speeded up or helped if you are given expert assistance from a teacher-coach or manager, or you may speed up the progress of young players by utilizing effective instructional and management procedures.

Instructional Objectives

You will be able to—

1. plan and provide meaningful learning experiences,
2. improve the individual and team play of performers, and
3. organize and conduct team play to maximize opportunities to win.

Often, experienced players wish to coach or manage a team. School-based programs will usually require a teaching certificate.

Respect for and acceptance of the manager-coach are essential and are fostered through demonstrated knowledge of the game and firm but fair treatment of the players. A successful manager-coach accurately diagnoses the needs of the player and prescribes meaningful learning experiences. In addition, good judgment, a sense of humor, and a positive self-concept are important personal traits that can inspire the desire to learn and the will to succeed.

Planning

Instructional plans are usually based on the age, ability, and interest of the learner. Following is a suggested progression of skills for various age groups.

Managing Duties

The manager-coach or the manager is responsible for the overall operation of the team, which includes the selection of the team, conditioning, instruction, and conduct of the game. As a coach or manager, you must have not only a thorough knowledge of your team but also of the opposition. This knowledge will assist you in deciding lineups, pitching changes, pinch hitters, runners, and fielding maneuvers. Decisions need to be made and communicated to the team concerning

Elementary School	Junior High School	High School and College
Throwing	Batting: grips, bunting	Batting: hit-and-run, fake bunting, drag bunting, place hitting
Catching	Baserunning: leadoff, stealing bases	
Fielding		Baserunning: rounding, sliding
Running	Throwing: overhand, sidearm, underhand	Throwing: sidearm, cutoff
Batting		Fielding: charging, reading conditions
Basic rules	Fielding: grounders, fly balls, backing, use of mitt and glove, tagging	
Leadup games		Strategy
	Position play: covering area, duties	Patterns of play
		Official rules: advanced rules
	Official rules	Umpiring
	Slow-pitch game	
	Soft-softball fast-pitch game	

(1) their defensive positions, (2) where a play is to be made, (3) the likelihood of a bunt or steal, (4) plans to steal, and so forth. These decisions will be based upon a careful analysis of the following points:

Pitcher: control, style, "stuff," and fielding ability
Catcher: throwing ability, agility, alertness, and backing of first base
Infielders: position, throwing ability, covering, and backing excellence
Outfielders: field condition, speed, and throwing ability

Promote improved play by reviewing the game with the team immediately after completion. Compliment good play but avoid placing blame and criticizing mistakes. Explain proper actions and prescribe special help and practice for consistent performance failures. (See figure 10.1.)

Team Selection

You should select team members on the following bases: (1) apparent natural ability as demonstrated by ease and correctness when throwing, fielding, and hitting, (2) speed and hitting, (3) strong and accurate throwing, (4) dependability and dedication, and (5) team needs. Although all of these criteria are important, dependability and dedication can transform a below-average player into one possessing acceptable abilities.

Conditioning

Getting the team ready for play requires preseason conditioning and pregame warm-up. *Preseason conditioning* should include several weeks of flexibility, strength, and endurance training. As a general rule, players should at least three times a week do static stretches in all muscle groups; progressively overload the

Figure 10.1
Team meeting.

capacity of the major muscle groups by increasing sets of exercises, the repetitions, and the load; and run a mile. The *pregame warm-up* should include loosening up arms and legs by stretching, throwing, and running. Infielders need practice in fielding grounders from their positions and throwing to various bases. The outfielders should practice catching fly balls and line drives and returning throws. The pitcher needs several minutes of progressively more demanding and accurate practice.

Instruction

Instruction should be the major goal of practice. The amount of practice depends upon the level of play and age of the players. Usually teams will practice from three to five days a week for two to three hours. It is important to adhere to the following principles to guide instruction and practice:

1. Plan each practice to make the most of the time.
2. Secure one coach or teacher for every four or five players.
3. Plan to keep all players active and busily engaged in improving their play.
4. Vary the practice to include new skills and yet have sufficient repetition to reinforce skills.
5. Emphasize defensive practice early in the season and offensive practice later. Organize offensive practice to minimize inactivity.

Conduct of Practice

Individual and group practice drills and tasks have been suggested in earlier chapters. Maximize practice as much as possible. You should work with the learner to identify specific goals to be achieved.

Preseason practice should begin four to six weeks before the schedule begins. Early meetings should stress conditioning, light throwing, and running. A typical practice session may be as follows:

Warm-ups and conditioning	15 minutes
Review and practice skills	10–30 minutes
Plan individual and group tasks with identified goals.	
Batting practice	60 minutes
Pitchers rotate every 20 minutes.	
Fielders play position and make directed plays.	
Batters are directed to hit a certain number of hits.	
Specific skill practice is conducted.	
Infield and outfield practice	15 minutes
Game play	20–30 minutes
Play bunt game.	

The ball is batted over the left fielder's head. What directions should the first base coach be giving to the batter–base runner? Why?

Conduct of the Game

As soon as possible inform the players of the starting lineup. Always look ahead to your team and the opponent's next hitters to plan any needed substitutions. Direct the coaches as to offensive strategy and the fielders as to defensive strategy. React positively to events good or bad and communicate with players concerning their feelings and ideas. Project a winning attitude and be sure you know the rules. After the game discuss with the team their successes and failures.

Coaching Duties

The rules permit one member of the offensive team to stand at the sidelines by first base and another by third base. These coaches may be players, coaches, managers, or other personnel connected with the team. They must not interfere with play, but they may direct the batting and running activities of the team.

The coaches shout words of encouragement to the batter and give the batter directions by the use of certain words or signs. Coaches assist the base runners in the proper running of the bases by shouting directions to them (see figure 10.2). A good coach must be able to make quick decisions. The coach assumes a position in the coach's box that will permit him or her to see the runners and fielders easily. Coaches give signs to the batter and direct his or her running on the base. The third base coach usually gives the signs to the batter. Keep the same sign for a particular

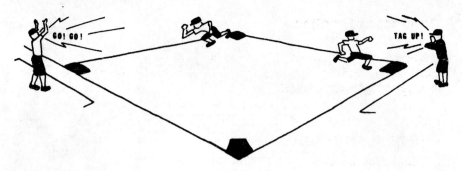

Figure 10.2
Using coaches.

action but vary preceding and succeeding signs. This will confuse the opposition but not your team. Signals include touching the ear, chin, nose, or belt buckle or placing hands together, on the knees, head, and so forth.

Safety

The following basic rules will help to ensure the safety of everyone playing softball:

1. Teach proper sliding techniques, since this skill accounts for the most injuries.
2. Plan adequate conditioning program and pregame warm-up.
3. Arrange practice drills so that batted or thrown balls will not hit performers.
4. Arrange practice so that each team is seated at least twenty feet behind home plate and behind the foul line.
5. Use bases that are recessed or have a quick release.
6. Rehabilitate an injury before resuming play.

References

ASA Softball. Oklahoma City, OK: Amateur Softball Association (nationally circulated magazine).

Balls and Strikes. Oklahoma City, OK: Amateur Softball Association (monthly newspaper).

Craig, Susan, and Ken Johnson. *The Softball Book*. West Point, NY: Leisure Press, 1984, Chapters 15 and 16.

Elliott, M. S., and Martha Ewing. *Youth Softball*. Dubuque, IA: Brown & Benchmark Publishers, 1992.

Houseworth, Steven D., and Francine V. Rivkin. *Coaching Softball Effectively*. Champaign, IL: Human Kinetics Publishers, Inc., 1985, Chapters 2 and 7.

Johnson, Carol Peterson with Margie Wright. *The Woman's Softball Book*. New York, NY: Leisure Press, 1984, Chapter 1.

Messler, Stephan P., and Mary Ann Brady. "The Mechanics of Batting: A Brief Review of Current Research." *1985–87 Softball Guide*. National Association for Girls' and Women's Sports, Reston, VA: American Alliance for Health, Physical Education and Dance.

Meyer, Robert G. *The Complete Book of Softball*. New York, NY: Leisure Press, 1984, Chapter 1.

National Association for Girls' and Women's Sport. *Softball Guide,* Washington, D.C.: American Alliance for Health, Physical Education and Recreation (published biannually).

Potter, Diane, and Gretchen Brockmeyer. *Softball—Steps to Success*. Champaign, IL: Leisure Press, 1989.

Reach, J., and B. Schwartz. *Softball Everyone*. Chapel Hill, NC: Hunter Textbooks, Inc., 1989.

Rikli, Roberta E., editor. *Softball Skills Test Manual*. Reston, VA: American Association for Health, Physical Education, Recreation and Dance, 1991.

Softball Rules Guide. Oklahoma City, OK: Amateur Softball Association (published yearly).

Umpire Rules and Case Book. Oklahoma City, OK: Amateur Softball Association (published yearly).

Walker, June. "Selected Outfield Techniques." *1985–87 Softball Guide*. Reston, VA: National Association for Girls' and Women's Sports of the American Alliance for Health, Physical Education, Recreation and Dance, pp. 17–20.

Wenk, Robert. *Coaching Youth Softball*. West Point, NY: Leisure Press, 1984, Chapter 15.

Questions and Answers

Multiple Choice

1. What is the major difference between fast-pitch softball and slow-pitch softball?
   a. none
   b. more offensive plan in fast pitch
   c. more offensive play in slow pitch
   d. more offensive play in fast pitch   (Ch. 1)
2. How old is the game of softball?
   a. over 100 years
   b. more than 75 but less than 100
   c. more than 50 but less than 75
   d. more than 25 but less than 50   (Ch. 1)
3. Where is the best position for the second baseman to stand when no one is on the base?
   a. on second base
   b. between first and second bases, about fifteen feet toward first base from second base
   c. between first and second bases, slightly closer to first base
   d. between first and second bases, halfway between first and second base   (Ch. 5)
4. Who is responsible for catching a fly ball between the infielders and outfielders?
   a. outfielders   c. whoever calls for it
   b. infielders   d. the fastest runners   (Ch. 5)
5. There are less than two outs with runners on first and second base. The batter hits a fly ball to the infield. What is the decision concerning the batter?
   a. becomes a base runner   c. automatically takes first base
   b. called out   d. continues to bat   (Ch. 7)
6. Where does the short fielder position himself/herself in slow-pitch softball?
   a. in the infield near second base
   b. between the left and center fielder
   c. between the right and center fielder
   d. in the infield between the shortstop and second base
   e. where the team prefers or situation warrants   (Ch. 5)
7. Who backs up the catcher when there is a play at home plate?
   a. third baseman   c. first baseman
   b. pitcher   d. second baseman   (Ch. 5)

133

8. Who should back up the first baseman when a ground ball is hit to the second baseman with no base runners on base?
   a. pitcher
   b. second baseman
   c. right fielder
   d. catcher (Ch. 5)
9. What is the name of the player who may play anywhere in the field in slow-pitch softball?
   a. designated hitter
   b. extra hitter
   c. extra fielder
   d. short fielder (Ch. 1)
10. What position should the infield be playing when there is a runner on third base with less than two outs?
    a. back position
    b. halfway position
    c. close-in position
    d. bunt position (Ch. 6)
11. When may both fast- and slow-pitch base runners advance to the next base but with liability to be put out?
    a. after a fly ball is caught
    b. after a base on balls
    c. after ball leaves the pitcher's hand
    d. anytime (Ch. 7)
12. Who must wear batting helmets?
    a. all adult fast-pitch and Junior Olympic fast- and slow-pitch offensive players
    b. all players in both fast- and slow-pitch softball
    c. only fast-pitch players
    d. no one, since it is optional (Ch. 1)
13. In fast pitch, where should the third baseman stand when a bunt is expected?
    a. on base path from second base
    b. near third base
    c. one-third in from base to home plate
    d. halfway from third base to home plate (Ch. 5)
14. What regulations distinguish slow-pitch softball from fast-pitch softball?
    a. ball size
    b. no differences
    c. moderate speed and at least a six-foot arc on slow-pitched balls
    d. diamond dimensions (Ch. 5)
15. What position should the infield be playing when there is a runner on first base and less than two outs?
    a. back position
    b. halfway position
    c. close-in position
    d. bunt position (Ch. 6)
16. Where should a right-handed player attempt to contact the ball to place hit to right field?
    a. opposite the body
    b. in front of the body
    c. behind the body
    d. doesn't matter (Ch. 3)
17. Which procedure should be followed to pitch an upshoot or rise in fast-pitch play?
    a. snap wrist right
    b. snap wrist left
    c. snap wrist down
    d. snap wrist upward (Ch. 5)

18. What name was given to softball when it was first developed?
    a. Kittenball
    b. One old cat
    c. Rounders
    d. Bat ball
    e. Slow pitch   (Ch. 2)

19. Where is the Softball Hall of Fame located?
    a. Peoria, Illinois
    b. Oklahoma City, Oklahoma
    c. Boston, Massachusetts
    d. Orange, California   (Ch. 2)

20. In slow-pitch play, the batter bunts on a 1–1 count the ball in fair territory.
    What is the umpire's decision?
    a. batter is out
    b. foul ball
    c. a strike is called
    d. a ball is called   (Ch. 7)

21. In fast-pitch play, the base runner leaves the base before the pitcher's nonpivot
    foot crosses the front edge of the pitcher's plate. What is the umpire's decision?
    a. legal, base runner is safe
    b. illegal, base runner is out
    c. illegal, ball is called on the batter
    d. depends on what the batter does to the pitch   (Ch. 7)

22. A batted ball bounces in the infield and then rolls outside the baseline. What
    is the decision of the umpire?
    a. strike
    b. out
    c. fair ball
    d. foul ball   (Ch. 7)

23. What is the minimum number of innings to be completed for an official game?
    a. seven
    b. six
    c. four
    d. five   (Ch. 7)

24. The batter has one strike and two balls when he/she tips the next pitch, which
    is caught by the catcher. What is the decision of the umpire?
    a. strike
    b. out
    c. fair ball
    d. foul ball   (Ch. 7)

25. The catcher drops the ball on the third strike. Bases are full and there is one
    out. What is the umpire's decision?
    a. strike
    b. out
    c. foul ball
    d. ball   (Ch. 7)

26. What is the umpire's signal for suspending play?
    a. extend both arms above the head
    b. raise right hand upward
    c. extend both arms diagonally in front of body
    d. extend arm in a pumping motion   (Ch. 9)

27. What action should a right-handed batter take to place hit the ball to left field?
    a. contact ball opposite body and follow through naturally
    b. contact the ball a little past the center of body and follow through toward right
       field
    c. contact the ball anywhere over the plate and swing fast with a full follow-through
    d. contact the ball in front of the body, "break" wrists sharply to cause a forceful
       follow-through   (Ch. 3)

28. Where is the strike zone for fast-pitch softball?
    a. between the shoulders and ankles and over the plate
    b. no higher than the neck and no lower than the knees and over the plate
    c. between armpits and knees over the plate
    d. between armpits and the knees   (Ch. 1)
29. What should a fielder do to avoid running into a fence when catching a fly ball near it?
    a. reach for fence with nonglove hand
    b. reach for fence with glove hand
    c. look back for the fence while moving back
    d. concentrate only on catching the ball   (Ch. 4)
30. How many bases may a base runner advance on an overthrow over the third baseman's head into fair territory?
    a. one   c. as many as possible
    b. two   d. none of these   (Ch. 3)
31. What action should be taken to correct a tendency to strike out by missing the ball?
    a. shorten grip and watch the ball closely
    b. shorten grip and adjust stride
    c. lengthen grip and swing faster
    d. lengthen grip and adjust stride   (Ch. 3)
32. Which fast-pitch delivery makes a complete circle for the windup?
    a. straight pitch   c. windmill
    b. slingshot   d. rocker   (Ch. 4)
33. Where do the coaches stand to help the offense?
    a. anywhere in foul territory   c. by the manager
    b. they must sit on the bench   d. on the sidelines by first and
                                                 third base   (Ch. 8)
34. What is the correct movement for a right-handed person in executing an overhand throw?
    a. stand with left shoulder toward person to whom the ball is going and step ahead
       on the left foot
    b. stand with the left shoulder toward the person to whom the ball is to be thrown
       and step ahead on the right foot
    c. stand facing the person to whom the ball is to be thrown and step ahead on the left
       foot
    d. stand any way that is comfortable and step ahead on either foot   (Ch. 4)
35. Where should the hands usually be placed on the bat for power hitting?
    a. both hands close together at the end of the bat
    b. hands separated about two inches apart, but near the end of the bat
    c. hands separated, about three inches from end of the bat
    d. hands close together about two or three inches from the end of the bat   (Ch. 3)

36. Which is the correct method to use in fielding ground balls?
    a. wait for the ball to roll to you
    b. run forward to meet the ball and try to field it on the first bounce
    c. run forward to meet the ball, but wait until the ball has slowed down to assist in stopping it
    d. creep up on the ball slowly (Ch. 4)
37. How should a fielder catch a fly ball that is going over his/her head?
    a. run backward and keep eye on the ball
    b. wait until the ball has landed and then run to pick it up
    c. let the player behind you catch it
    d. turn around and run toward the direction the ball is headed, keep eye on the ball (Ch. 4)
38. How should the batting order be selected?
    a. let the team decide
    b. according to the positions played on the team
    c. according to the batting skill of the batters
    d. pitcher, catcher, then the weakest hitters next (Ch. 6)
39. What is the term used for the next batter to bat?
    a. batter up   c. on-deck batter
    b. clean-up hitter   d. leadoff hitter (Ch. 2)
40. Which grip on the bat will provide the most power?
    a. long   c. choke
    b. medium   d. depends on the batter (Ch. 3)
41. What action listed below will help to correct hitting only ground balls?
    a. swing up on the ball   c. swing level at the ball
    b. swing down on the ball   d. swing harder at the ball (Ch. 3)
42. How should the batter adjust his/her position when the ball leaves the pitcher's hand?
    a. relax   c. shift weight to rear foot
    b. hold position   d. shift weight to forward foot (Ch. 3)
43. When playing fast-pitch softball, which type of pitch is easiest to bunt? (Right-handed batter)
    a. high outside   d. low inside
    b. low outside   e. high inside (Ch. 3)
    c. in the middle
44. What is the correct method to round a base?
    a. swing wide before reaching the base and touch any part of the bag
    b. run straight to the base, touch the inside corner and pivot body around
    c. curve out a bit several feet from the base and touch the inside corner
    d. get there any way possible (Ch. 3)
45. Which slide provides the smallest tag area?
    a. straight-in   c. hook
    b. bent-leg   d. headfirst (Ch. 3)

46. Which slide is best to avoid being tagged?
    a. straight-in
    b. bent-leg
    c. hook
    d. any of the above (Ch. 3)
47. What position should your hands be in to field or catch a ball below your waist?
    a. thumbs together
    b. little fingers together
    c. left hand only, palm up
    d. hand with glove on it, facing upward (Ch. 4)
48. What is the correct position for fielding a ground ball? (Right-handed player)
    a. brace feet apart with left foot ahead, bend knees and hips
    b. bend only from the waist
    c. brace feet apart with right foot ahead, bend knees and hips
    d. bend from knees and hips only (Ch. 4)
49. What is the best body position for a tag play?
    a. straddle the bag, place gloved hand in front of base
    b. stay to one side of base and tag runner
    c. brace feet apart behind the base and reach for the runner
    d. block the base with the left foot and tag the runner (Ch. 4)
50. What is the advantage of an overhand throw?
    a. the throw can be done faster
    b. more accurate for a short distance
    c. speed and power are best
    d. throw can be delivered sooner (Ch. 4)

True or False

51. Softball playing field dimensions for pitching, infield and outfield size vary depending upon the type, level, and gender of play. False (Ch. 1)
52. Legal bats can be made of plastic. False (Ch. 1)
53. Pitchers have priority over all fly balls that travel across several positions in the infield. (Ch. 6)
54. The first option of the defensive layers involved in a rundown play is to outrun and tag out the base runner. False True (Ch. 5)
55. In sixteen-inch slow-pitch play, the pitcher may attempt to pick off a base runner who is leading off. True (Ch. 7)
56. A passed ball is a pitched ball that the batter does not attempt to swing at. (Ch. 2)
57. Managers are in charge of the team. (Ch. 10)
58. A foul ball and a foul tip are the same thing. (Ch. 2)
59. It is legal for the pitcher to start to pitch and then stop. (Ch. 2)
60. When attempting to throw out a base runner, throw the ball on the side away from the runner. True (Ch. 4)
61. If the pitcher hits the batter with a pitched ball, the batter is allowed to go to first base. (Fast-pitch play) True (Ch. 7)
62. The only time a base runner must be tagged out is when he/she is forced to run. True false (Ch. 7)

63. If a base runner is hit with a batted ball, he/she is out immediately. *True* (Ch. 7)
64. Base runners may run outside the base path to avoid being tagged. (Ch. 8)
65. Designated hitters (DH) are permitted only in slow-pitch play. *False* (Ch. 3)
66. Short fielders play in the infield or outfield. *True* (Ch. 5)
67. All official softballs are twelve inches in circumference. (Ch. 2)
68. There are special playing rules for coed softball. *True* (Ch. 7)
69. The ASA is the official rule-setting agency. *True* (Ch. 7)
70. An "extra hitter" in slow-pitch softball is a position similar to "designated
    hitter" in fast-pitch softball. *False True* (Ch. 1)
71. An outfielder should throw toward an infielder for a possible cutoff when a
    batter gets a hit with runners on base. *True* (Ch. 4)
72. Flexibility exercises are important to softball conditioning to lessen injuries.
    (Ch. 8)
73. Stealing a base is permitted in all types of softball play. *False* (Ch. 3)
74. You should never change your mind while in the act of sliding. (Ch. 6)
75. When no one is on base, the catcher should back up the first baseman on
    throws to first base. (Ch. 6)
76. Slow-pitch pitchers try to deceive batters by varying the height of the arc and
    hitting the corners of the plate. *True* (Ch. 5)
77. Catchers should always hold their mitt as a target in the middle of the plate.
    False True (Ch. 5)
78. "Giving" with the catch will prevent the ball from bouncing out of the glove
    or hands. *True* (Ch. 4)
79. Gripping the ball by the finger pads lessens throwing accuracy. *False* (Ch. 4)
80. When catching a ball thrown to a base with an advancing runner, catching
    position should be delayed to the last second. *True* (Ch. 4)

Completion

81. What type of conditioning exercises should a player perform? (Ch. 8)
82. What is the term applied to the catcher and pitcher? (Ch. 2)
83. What is the name of the organization that promotes softball in the United
    States? (Ch. 2)
84. What is the offensive play called when the base runner tries to advance at the
    same time the batter tries to hit the ball? (Ch. 3)
85. What two types of bunts are executed to achieve a base hit in fast-pitch play?
    (Ch. 5)
86. What is the term applied to a throw from the outfield to an infielder when the
    distance is too far to throw? *Pitcher* (Ch. 4)
87. Who covers home plate on a wild pitch with a runner on third base? (Ch. 4)
88. What should fielders do to shield their eyes from the sun if they have no
    sunglasses? *Use their glove* (Ch. 4)
89. What kind of a hit will a level swing produce? *Line Drive* (Ch. 3)

90. What action must be applied to the swing to deaden the ball for bunting? (Ch. 3)
91. List three factors that would determine whether you should steal a base while playing fast-pitch softball. (Ch. 3)
92. What are the two main purposes of executing a cutoff throw? (Ch. 5)
93. List three kinds of pitches. (Ch. 5)
94. Where should the outfielders play when a powerful right-handed batter is batting? (Ch. 6)
95. What is the difference between a safety and a suicide squeeze? (Ch. 6)
96. What is the term applied to gaining two outs on one batted ball? (Ch. 2)
97. What is the major purpose of a slide? (Ch. 3)
98. What conditions influence rule variations for softball play? (Ch. 9)
99. What is the visual signal that an umpire gives to indicate a "ball"? (Ch. 9)
100. Name three defensive positions for both slow- and fast-pitch softball. (Ch. 6)

Question Answer Key

Multiple Choice

1. c	6. e	11. a	16. c
2. a	7. b	12. a	17. d
3. b	8. d	13. d	18. a
4. a	9. d	14. c	19. b
5. b	10. c	15. b	20. a
21. b	26. a	31. a	36. b
22. d	27. d	32. c	37. d
23. d	28. c	33. d	38. c
24. a	29. a	34. a	39. c
25. b	30. c	35. a	40. a
41. c	46. c		
42. c	47. b		
43. b	48. a		
44. c	49. a		
45. d	50. c		

True or False

51. T	57. T	63. T	69. T	75. T
52. T	58. F	64. F	70. T	76. T
53. F	59. F	65. F	71. T	77. F
54. T	60. T	66. T	72. T	78. T
55. T	61. T	67. F	73. F	79. F
56. F	62. F	68. T	74. T	80. T

Completion

81. flexibility, strength
82. battery
83. ASA
84. hit-and-run
85. drag and push
86. relay
87. pitcher
88. use glove
89. line drive
90. give
91. speed, no. of outs, kind of batter, ability of defense, score
92. to stop the runner from advancing and to throw out a base runner
93. curve, drop, fast, rise, knuckleball, change-up
94. back to left
95. The third baseman can return to third base on a safety squeeze but must continue to run to home plate on a suicide squeeze.
96. double play
97. avoid tag
98. age, gender, and type of play
99. none
100. close in, halfway, back

Index

Kampschmidt, Bernie, 13
Keystone sack, 17
Kirkendall, Dizzy, 13
Korgan, Nina, 14

Language of softball, 11–19
Law, Marjorie, 14
Laws, unwritten, 108–9
Lay one down, 17
Leading off, 94
Lead off, 17, 38–39
Leaping, 17
Left fielder, 88
Legal touch, 17
Lettuce, 7
Lewis, Daywell, 7
Linde, Al, 13
Line drive, 17
Lopiano, Donna, 14
Lore, of softball, 11–19

Managing, and coaching, 125–29
Masks, 7, 17
May, Gloria, 14
Miller, Clarence, 13
Mimetic footwork, 85
Mimetic pitching, 73
Mitts, 7

National Association for Girls' and Women's
    Sports (NAGWS), 9, 107
National Association for Sport and
    Physical Education, 9
National Federation of High School
    Activities Association, 9
National Health Care Discount, 12
National Recreation Association, 12
National Softball Hall of Fame, 9, 13
Nutritional conditioning, 113–14

Obstruction, 17
Offensive patterns, 91–94
Offensive skills, 21–42
Official rules, 101–7
Officiating, 107
Olympics, 8
On deck batter, 17
One Old Cat, 11
Out, 17
Outfield, 2, 17
Outfielder evaluation form, 86
Outfielders, 87–88
Outside pitch, 17
Overhand snap, 59

Overhand throw, 57–59
Overrun, 17
Over slide, 17
Overthrow, 17

Pan American Games, 8
Pass, 17
Passed balls, 17
Patterns of play, 91–100
Pauley, M. J., 12
Pepper, 33
Peralta, Amy, 14
Physical conditioning, 112–13
Picking off, 80
Pickoff, 17
Pinch hitter, 18
Pinch runner, 18
Pitcher, 2–3, 65–73
Pitcher's plate, 8
Pitches, types of, 70–71
Pitching
    fast-pitch, 65–70
    grips, 70–71
    mimetic, 73
    problems and corrections, 73
    rules, 65–66, 104
    slow-pitch, 71
Pitching regulations, 65–66, 104
Pitchout, 18
Pivot and throw, 85
Pivot foot, 18
Place-hitting, 26–27
Planning, 125–26
Plate umpire, 116–17
Play
    competitive, 111–14
    patterns of, 91–100
Play, the game, 111–14
Players, and substitutes, 103
Play field, 2, 101–3
Pop flies, 70
Pop-ups, 18
Porter, Don, 8
Position play, defensive, 65–90
Pregame warmup, 127
Preplan, 60
Preseason conditioning, 126
Priority plays, 99–100
Protectors, 7
Protest, 18
Psychological conditioning, 114
Pulled-in position, 95–96
Pull hitter, 18